· KITCHEN METRICS ·

For cooking and baking convenience, the Metric Commission of Canada suggests the following for adapting to metric measurement. The table gives approximate, rather than exact, conversions.

· SPOONS ·

¼ teaspoon = 1 milliliter
½ teaspoon = 2 milliliters
1 teaspoon = 5 milliliters
1 tablespoon = 15 milliliters
2 tablespoons = 25 milliliters
3 tablespoons = 50 milliliters

· CUPS ·

¼ cup = 50 milliliters
⅓ cup = 75 milliliters
½ cup = 125 milliliters
⅔ cup = 150 milliliters
¾ cup = 175 milliliters
1 cup = 250 milliliters

· OVEN TEMPERATURES ·

200°F	=	100°C	350°F = 180°C	
225°F	=	110°C	375°F = 190°C	
250°F	=	120°C	400°F = 200°C	
275°F	=	140°C	425°F = 220°C	
300°F	=	150°C	450°F = 230°C	
325°F	=	160°C	475°F = 240°C	

BREAKFAST & BRUNCH
Book

BREAKFAST & BRUNCH
Book

NORMAN KOLPAS

HPBooks
A division of
PRICE STERN SLOAN

A FRIEDMAN GROUP BOOK

Menus and recipes from the Ritz-Carlton, Boston, Arnaud's,
Michael's, and The Four Seasons are printed with permission
from those restaurants.

HPBooks
A division of Price Stern Sloan, Inc.
360 North La Cienega Boulevard
Los Angeles, California 90048

Library of Congress Cataloging-in-Publication Data

Kolpas, Norman.
  Breakfast & brunch book.

  Includes index.
  1. Breakfasts. 2. Brunches. I. Title. II. Title:
Breakfast and brunch book.
TX733.K65   1988   641.5'3   87-24852
ISBN 0-89586-616-1

BREAKFAST & BRUNCH BOOK
was prepared and produced by
Michael Friedman Publishing Group, Inc.
15 West 26th Street
New York, New York 10010

Editor: Nancy Kalish
Art Director: Mary Moriarty
Designer: Liz Trovato
Photo Editor: Christopher Bain
Production Manager: Karen L. Greenberg

Typeset by B.P.E. Graphics
Color separations by Hong Kong Scanner Craft Company Ltd.
Printed and bound in Hong Kong by Leefung-Asco Printers Ltd.

· A C K N O W L E D G E M E N T S ·

I am indebted to Michael Friedman and Karla Olson for proposing to me the original idea for this book. Nancy Kalish was not merely an attentive and thorough editor; she was an enthusiastic supporter, and a joy to work with.

My wife, Katie, made the work easier at home with her love of adventurous new breakfasts. In spirit, this book is as much hers as it is mine.

C O N T E N T S

C O N T E N T S

DiMicco/Ferris

INTRODUCTION

More and more of us are finally learning what our mothers knew all along: No meal is more important than the morning meal.

A good, hearty, well-balanced breakfast or brunch gives you the nutrients you need to start the day at your best. Hot drinks help wake us. Fresh fruit provides a burst of energy, and complex carbohydrates in breads or cereals keep that energy coming. Finally, the protein from eggs, dairy products, and breakfast meats keeps our bodies strong.

But there's more to the morning meal than just its foods. A good morning meal, beautifully presented, cheers us. A bountiful breakfast set out on the dining room table is the perfect way to gather the family together. A weekend buffet brunch is a great way to entertain. A ''power breakfast'' for colleagues could help you achieve an important business goal. A solitary breakfast of favorite, comforting foods could be a time for important reflection. Breakfast, in short, feeds the soul as well as the body.

This book celebrates the benefits breakfast and brunch offer to both body and soul. It begins with Breakfast & Brunch Basics, a comprehensive survey of morning ingredients: fruits and juices; cereals; breads and muffins; pastries; pancakes, waffles, and French toasts; eggs; seafood, poultry, and meats; vegetables; dairy products; and hot beverages. In each chapter, you'll find preparation tips and basic recipes, along with elaborations and variations. Next, Table Settings offers guidelines for tableware essentials, along with ideas for setting a mood through your choices in dishes and accessories, tablecloths, napkins and placemats, and other decorative elements.

Finally, you'll find a collection of breakfast and brunch menus, each of which combines an occasion with appropriate recipes and table-setting suggestions. As a bonus, there are special menus from four outstanding restaurants—The Four Seasons in New York, The Ritz-Carlton Hotel in Boston, Arnaud's in New Orleans, and Michael's in Los Angeles—that will enable you to create their acclaimed specialties in your own kitchen.

Let this book open your eyes to the many delicious possibilities that breakfast and brunch afford us. I hope you will use it not just as a guide, but also as a starting point for creating your own exciting morning meals. Mom would be proud of you!

—Norman Kolpas

BREAKFAST & BRUNCH BASICS

FRUITS & JUICES

Nothing starts the day off more brightly than fresh fruit or a glass of freshly squeezed juice. The taste is light, clean, sprightly; fruit or juice moistens and cools a dry morning throat, and its natural sugar gives a still-sluggish body its first surge of energy.

That's why, more often than not, breakfasts begin with fruit or juice. Fruits and juices literally wake up the palate—and the digestion—to the meal that follows.

Vern Green

· CHOOSING FRUITS ·

You can serve virtually any fruit at breakfast. It's really just a matter of personal taste—and what you're up to facing first thing in the morning! For example, I love apples, and I know plenty of people who love to eat them in the morning, but their snappy crispness is just a bit too brash for me at that time of day. And bananas seem a bit heavy all on their own, though I often eat them whole at lunchtime and I enjoy them sliced on cereal or whipped up in fruit juice smoothies.

You, like me, may well prefer one of the juicier fruits. Citrus fruits are terrific with their zippy, fresh flavors, and so are melons, berries, and seedless grapes. They quench a morning thirst as neatly as anything you might drink. And most spectacular of all are the wide range of tropical fruits that modern shipping and storage are making available virtually year-round and worldwide, bringing exotic tastes to the breakfast table.

· JUICES: A GROWING · RANGE OF CHOICES

The citrus fruits are logical first choices: it's easy to extract the juice and there's lots of it. But a wide variety of other juices are available commercially: apple juice, which is now, happily, sold in pure, unfiltered form, a much more delicious drink than the clear, filtered kind; grape juice, both red and white varieties; pineapple juice; prune juice; and cranberry juice, a tart alternative that requires sweetening or blending with a sweeter juice. And though I've never had a taste for it in the morning, there's always tomato juice.

Beyond these basics, many supermarkets—and especially food stores specializing in gourmet and

health foods—now carry a wide array of juices such as kiwi, papaya, strawberry, mango, watermelon, and cantaloupe, as well as thicker-textured blends (sometimes called smoothies), incorporating anything from coconut milk to blueberries to bananas. This kind of variety is now within the reach of home kitchens, too, with the help of specialized juicers, food processors, and blenders. It's worth making the small investment in one of these machines, if you at all value the vibrant flavor (not to mention the nutritional benefits) of freshly squeezed juice.

Chuck Keeler Jr./Manhattan Views

MELONS—MYRIAD BLESSINGS

A shopper in search of melons for the breakfast table has many a blessing to count; each year seems to bring a wider variety to the produce department. And understandably so, when you learn that all the many varieties (apart from the watermelon) belong to the same species and cross-pollinate like mad; growers have to keep separate varieties at least a quarter of a mile (.4 kilometers) apart. Nevertheless, melons can be divided into three basic groups: the musk melons, the winter melons, and, standing alone in a separate species, the watermelons.

Brian Leatart

· MUSK MELONS ·

The name comes logically from the rich, spicy perfume given off by these melons, a scent that grows heavier as they ripen. Best-known of this variety is the orange-fleshed cantaloupe; its close cousins include Persian melons and the green-fleshed Ogen melons. Another name for the group is "netted melons," which describes the characteristic net-like markings on their skins.

Good musk melons should have the characteristic sweet smell and feel heavy for their size. Their stem ends should have clean, slightly concave scars, a sign of vine-ripening. A ripe melon will have lost most of its green color, and will yield slightly to pressure at the stem end.

· WINTER MELONS ·

Melons in this group, including casabas and honeydews, have hard, smooth, greenish skins and pale-green flesh that tends to be moister and less dense than musk melons. Because of their hard skins, they keep longer than musk melons and don't give off any discernible aroma.

A ripe winter melon will have a slight yellow tinge to its skin, and, though firm, will yield slightly to pressure.

· SERVING MUSK · & WINTER MELONS

Melons are best served slightly chilled—cool enough to refresh, yet not so cold that their taste is muted. If they've been refrigerated, let them stand at room temperature for about half an hour before serving; if already at room temperature, refrigerate them for about an hour.

Small melons are most simply served cut in half, seeded, and snugly placed in a bowl or with a thin slice cut off the rounded bottoms to allow them to sit securely on a serving plate. Cut larger melons into wedges after halving and seeding them. For a fancier presentation, carefully cut between the flesh and rind of the melon wedge to remove the flesh in one piece. Place the flesh back on the rind and cut the flesh crosswise into 1-inch (2½-centimeter) pieces; then gently slide each piece slightly sideways, alternating left and right, to create a decorative arrangement.

• GARNISHING MELONS •

A good melon has all the flavor it needs. But some people enjoy the sharp contrast of a squeeze of fresh lemon or lime. It was an old Middle Eastern custom to sprinkle melon with freshly ground pepper or grated ginger, a habit that may sound strange but can result in a startlingly delicious contrast of tastes (see recipe).

Deep-colored berries also make attractive garnishes for the pale-fleshed melons. Cantaloupe halves make especially beautiful containers for sliced strawberries or fresh blueberries.

• WATERMELONS •

Though watermelon is more often served as a summertime dessert, it makes a refreshing change of pace for breakfast. Choose a melon that sounds hollow when tapped and has an evenly colored green rind (though there are some special varieties of watermelon with striped green-and-white skins, or even all-white). Serve it well chilled, cut into small wedges. If you don't wish to bother breakfasters with seeds, cut the flesh of the melon into 1-inch (2½-centimeter) cubes, or scoop it with a melon-baller and carefully remove the seeds with a fork or the tip of a small, sharp knife.

O precious food! Delight of the mouth!
O! much better than gold, masterpiece of Apollo!
O flower of all the fruits! O ravishing melon!

—Marc Antoine de Saint-Amant (ca. 1580)

GINGERED CANTALOUPE WITH HONEY

The combination of spicy ginger and sweet, mellow honey seems to amplify the rich perfume of a good, ripe cantaloupe.

2 ripe cantaloupes, halved, seeded, and scooped with a melon-baller

1½ tablespoons honey

1 teaspoon finely grated fresh ginger

1 teaspoon freshly squeezed lemon juice

Put the cantaloupe balls in a large mixing bowl. Add the honey, ginger, and lemon juice and toss gently to coat the melon. Cover with plastic wrap and chill in the refrigerator for about 1 hour. Stir well before serving in small bowls.

Makes 6 to 8 servings.

CRÈME FRAÎCHE FOR BREAKFAST BERRIES

Berries are delicious on their own at breakfast, but a touch of cream makes them truly luxurious. Serve the heaviest, richest cream you can find, or lightly beat whipping cream, just until it thickens but is still pourable. Better yet, serve them with a dollop of French-style crème fraîche—a thick, fresh cream with an ever-so-slight tang reminiscent of yogurt. Many gourmet markets and delicatessens now sell crème fraîche, but you can make a very similar product at home.

1 cup whipping cream

1 tablespoon plain yogurt

In a jar with a tight-fitting lid, stir together the cream and yogurt. Close the lid, wrap the jar in a kitchen towel, and leave it at warm room temperature overnight.

Before serving, place the jar in the refrigerator to chill for about 1 hour. Stir well before serving.

Makes about 1¼ cups.

> ***The flesh of the pineapple melts into water and it is so flavorful that one finds in it the aroma of the peach, the apple, the quince, and the muscat grape. I can call it with justice the king of fruits because it is the most beautiful and best of all those of the earth.***
>
> **—Père du Tertre (1595)**

RARE TREASURES

Try starting your breakfast with an exotic flourish by serving one of the following unusual fruits. Rarities until recently, many if not all of these can now be found for at least part of the year in large supermarkets.

CHERIMOYA

You'd never guess this heart-shaped fruit was edible from its brownish-green alligator-like skin. But cut it in half when it's ripe enough to yield to slight pressure, and you'll find an ivory-colored creamy-smooth interior (hence its alternate name, custard apple), perfect for eating with a spoon and riddled with large, inedible, shiny black seeds. The texture is amazing: When the fruit is very cold, it's like a fine sorbet. The flavor may remind you of pineapple, pears, apples, or none of these; let's face it, it tastes like a cherimoya. Look for them from late fall to spring.

CHINESE GRAPEFRUIT

If grapefruits have always been too acid for your taste, ask your grocer to track down this gargantuan, cantaloupe-sized variety, also called the pomelo. The skin *looks* like a grapefruit's and the segments inside are white, but the taste, though perfectly identifiable as that of a grapefruit, has absolutely none of the familiar sharp tang. Think of the difference between a really sour orange and a really sweet orange, and you'll get the idea.

Brian Leatart

Brian Leatart

KIWI

Originally called Chinese gooseberries, until a canny importer had the good sense to change the name to that of the national bird of the fruit's native land, New Zealand, these small fruits with their velvety-brown skins have grown enormously in popularity lately. Peeling reveals an almost fluorescent lime-green, juicy flesh with tiny black edible seeds. The refreshing taste has been compared to strawberries, pineapples, peaches, all of the above, or none of the above.

MANGO

My personal favorite. This oblong fruit is ready to eat when its thick skin has changed from green to blushing orange-red and yields slightly to the fingers. Inside is a bright orange, succulent flesh whose texture resembles that of a juicy peach and whose taste is wonderfully sweet and heady; at the center is a large, flat white seed from which you can suck the last bits of the fruit. No taste is more evocative of the tropics.

PAPAYA

For a tropical fruit, the gourd-shaped papaya is surprisingly mild in flavor, and it actually contains a natural enzyme that aids digestion—papain. Choose Hawaiian papayas over the larger, less sweet and succulent Mexican variety. They're ripe when their skin has changed from green to yellow-orange and they yield to slight pressure. Slice them in half lengthwise and scoop out and discard the black seeds at their center before serving. Serve with lime wedges.

TROPICAL FRUIT SALAD

Use this as the basis for fruit salads of your own devising. The secret with any fruit salad is not to go so overboard in the number of ingredients that the flavors and textures all blend together; you want each bite to be distinctive. For a special weekend breakfast you can add a few shots of orange-flavored Cointreau or Grand Marnier.

2 medium oranges, peeled, seeded, segments skinned and cut in half

2 bananas, peeled and cut into ¼-inch slices

2 kiwis, peeled, halved lengthwise, each half cut into ¼-inch slices

1 pineapple, peeled, cored, cut crosswise into ½-inch slices, each slice cut into 10 to 12 small pieces

1 mango, peeled, flesh sliced from seed and cut into ½-inch cubes

1 small lime, juiced

¼ cup shredded coconut

¼ cup Cointreau or Grand Marnier (optional)

2 teaspoons sugar

In a large mixing bowl, gently toss together all the ingredients, taking care not to break the more delicate fruits. Chill well before serving.

Makes 6 to 8 servings.

SPICED FRUIT COMPOTE

Especially on cold winter mornings, a dish of stewed dried fruit offers special comfort. Instead of water, you might like to simmer the fruits in apple juice for a richer flavor; if you do, cut the quantity of sugar in this recipe in half. Serve the fruits hot or cold.

½ cup small dried prunes

½ cup dried apricots

½ cup dried peaches

½ cup golden raisins

½ to ¾ cup sugar

2 whole cloves

1 cinnamon stick, broken into 3 pieces

1 thin slice fresh ginger

Put the fruits, sugar to taste, and the spices in a medium saucepan. Add enough cold water so that the fruits are submerged by ½ inch.

Bring the water to a boil. Then reduce the heat and simmer gently, covered, stirring occasionally, until the fruits are plump and tender—30 minutes to 1 hour, depending on how dry they were.

Before serving, taste the liquid and adjust the sweetness to your taste. Serve warm or chilled, accompanied, if you like, by heavy cream or Crème Fraîche (page 14).

Makes 2½ cups.

GETTING THE FRESHEST JUICE

Though supermarkets sell a fine array of fruit juices, you'll get the best taste and the most nutritional value if you make your own juice fresh each morning.

For citrus juices, the process is easy. Unless you're making breakfast for a crowd, all you need is an old-fashioned glass or plastic juicer on which you rotate cut citrus halves, the juice collecting in the receptacle beneath the ridged reamer. Electric juicers with rotating reamers speed up the job and keep your arm and wrist from tiring. Some juicers also include strainers to remove pulp, for those who don't like their juices chewy.

To make fresh juice from other fruits (apples, pineapples, grapes, melons, or tropical fruits) as well as tomato and vegetable juices (carrot, celery, and so on), you need to invest in a heavy-duty juice extractor. These motorized machines literally chew up whatever you put in them and squeeze out their essence. You're most likely to find them in well-stocked kitchenware shops and large health food stores.

Whatever device you use to make your morning juice, it's a good idea to pop the fruits into the refrigerator the night before, so your drink will come out chilled.

> ***A grapefruit is a lemon that had a chance and took advantage of it.***
>
> ***—Anonymous***

JUICE BLENDS

For greater variety, you might like to try blending together two or more different juices. Here are some complementary combinations. Use them as a starting point, varying the proportions and adding other juices to suit your own tastes.

APPLE-GRAPE
APPLE-KIWI
MIXED MELON
ORANGE-GRAPEFRUIT
PAPAYA-ORANGE
PINEAPPLE-GRAPEFRUIT
PINEAPPLE-KIWI
PINEAPPLE-ORANGE

Brian Leatart

SMOOTHIES

The key to a good smoothie is to select complementary flavors. Apple juice, orange juice, grape juice, and pineapple juice go well with other smoothie ingredients; they make good choices for the liquid portion. For whole fruit, select from bananas (they make the smoothest, most milkshake-like drinks), berries, peaches, melons, or tropical fruits. Some smoothie combinations also benefit from the addition of dried fruits—especially dates—and even peanut butter.

The proportions are basic: For 1 serving, use 1 cup of juice to 1 large whole piece of fruit (banana or peach) or ½ cup of smaller fruit (berries or chopped fruit); 2 dates and 1 tablespoon of peanut butter will be enough to add a rich flavor. If the smoothie seems too thick, just add a little more juice. You can double the quantities for 2 people, but do several batches if you're making smoothies for a crowd.

Put all the ingredients together in a blender or food processor and blend on high speed just until smooth—you don't want to beat too much air into the mixture. For a colder, frothier smoothie, peel and freeze the fruits the night before, or add a couple of ice cubes or ½ cup of crushed ice to the blender or processor (but take care: some food processors have trouble chopping up ice or hard-frozen fruit).

Below are some smoothie combinations to start you off.

APPLE-BANANA
APPLE-BANANA-DATE
APPLE-BANANA-DATE-PEANUT BUTTER
APPLE-BLUEBERRY
GRAPE-BANANA
GRAPE-PEACH
ORANGE-APRICOT
ORANGE-BANANA
ORANGE-STRAWBERRY
PINEAPPLE-BANANA
PINEAPPLE-PAPAYA

CEREALS & GRAINS

"Oats: a grain which in England is generally given to horses, but in Scotland supports the people." Thus did the great English man of letters, Dr. Johnson, tersely sum up the greatest of breakfast grains in his *Dictionary of the English Language.* Clearly, the good doctor's definition said more about the esteem in which he held Scotsmen than it did of his feelings about oats. He had probably never even tasted oatmeal, not wishing to stoop to the level of a beast of burden—*or* a Scot.

OATMEAL TOPPINGS

Any of the following toppings makes a great addition to oatmeal or other hot cooked cereals. Usually, you'll want one from each group: dairy; sweeteners; fruits, nuts, and grains. The truly self-indulgent start by burying a pat of butter in their oatmeal, and then add milk or cream and other toppings. If you're watching your weight, fresh fruit alone is wonderful.

For a special breakfast, especially when you're serving a large group, it's fun to put out a wide selection of toppings and let everyone pick and choose.

SWEETENERS

Granulated sugar
Brown sugar
Honey
Maple syrup
Molasses
Jams, jellies, or preserves
Chocolate chips (a major indulgence)

FRUITS, NUTS & GRAINS

Bananas (sliced)
Blueberries
Raspberries
Strawberries (sliced)
Peaches (sliced)
Raisins
Dates (pitted and chopped)
Shredded coconut
Almonds (slivered)
Cashews (coarsely chopped)
Hazelnuts (coarsely chopped)
Peanuts (coarsely chopped)
Granola
Wheat germ

DAIRY

Unsalted or salted butter
Skim, low-fat, or whole milk
Cream
Buttermilk
Plain or flavored yogurt

· A ·
STICK-TO-YOUR-RIBS
BREAKFAST

If he *had* bothered to taste oats, Dr. Johnson would have had no choice but to strike his definition from the manuscript. Nutlike, earthy, rich, and satisfying: all these adjectives apply to the oat and to the primary form it takes on the breakfast table—a thick oatmeal porridge. No breakfast food is more deliciously filling, more fortifying and sustaining. Served hot, straight from the saucepan and topped with milk or cream, butter, sugar, fresh fruit, or other embellishments, it provides a well-balanced breakfast that, as Mom promises on a cold winter morning, ''sticks to your ribs.''

Oats and other grains—especially wheat, corn, and rice—are some of the most widely eaten breakfast foods. Major supermarket space is given over to ready-to-eat products made from these grains—processed cereals, many of them chockfull of sugar and salt, artificial flavorings, and preservatives. Hundreds of millions of advertising dollars are spent on Saturday morning commercials aimed at brainwashing kids into begging their parents to buy the latest breakfast-in-a-box, resulting in close to 5 billion dollars a year in cereal sales in the U.S. alone.

· A HOMEMADE ·
CEREAL REBELLION

While some packaged cereals are quite simple and tasty, good cooks can rebel against the ersatz varieties and make their own cereals from scratch. It's so easy, and the results are so much more delicious—and *so much cheaper*—than anything you can buy in a cartoon-illustrated box, that I'm surprised more people don't.

Dried fruit-and-nut granola is easily made in advance in large quantities that keep well, ready for a fast breakfast or an impromptu snack. Likewise, a rich moist muesli made with grains and fresh fruits can be done the night before, and it takes just a few minutes to complete in the morning. Oatmeal (and I'm not talking about the quick-cooking kind that tastes like library paste) takes just about half an hour to prepare, and it doesn't need much attention while it cooks.

Made with whole grains, all of the homemade breakfast cereal recipes that follow have more of the essential dietary fiber (talked about so much these days) than the majority of commercial ''high fiber'' cereals. (For Southern-style grits, another cooked grain recipe served as a side dish, see page 68.) It takes so little effort to make a healthy breakfast cereal that really does stick to your ribs. Mother would be proud of you.

MFPG

SWISS MUESLI

This well-known cold cereal was invented by Dr. Bircher-Benner to supply the patients at his Swiss sanatorium with a healthy, well-rounded breakfast. If you like, you can add other fruits to it (but don't leave out the apples) and substitute yogurt for the cream.

¼ cup whole wheat berries

¼ cup whole oats

1 cup heavy cream

¼ cup honey

1 teaspoon lemon juice

3 apples, cored (skins left on) and coarsely grated

1 cup seedless green grapes, cut into halves

¼ cup toasted wheat germ

2 tablespoons slivered almonds

The night before serving, put the wheat and oats in a bowl and add cold water to cover them by about 1 inch. Loosely cover the bowl and leave the grains to soak overnight at room temperature.

The next morning, drain the grains thoroughly. In a mixing bowl, stir together the cream, honey, and lemon juice. Add the fruit. Stir in the wheat, oats, wheat germ, and almonds. Serve at once.

Makes 4 to 6 servings.

TOASTED WALNUT OATMEAL WITH BLUEBERRIES AND CREAM

I was brought up on oatmeal made from rolled oats—oats with their husks ground off, then steamed and flattened. It's a good product. Imagine my surprise, then, when I discovered that oats weren't flat and pale gray, but rather tiny grains the shape of rice, with nut-brown husks. These grains are ground into meal for cooking purposes: fine oatmeal is used for baking; coarse oatmeal (the pieces are often as big as half a grain) is used for porridge.

You can buy coarse oatmeal in most supermarkets. Just look for it, possibly shelved with flours and grains rather than with the breakfast cereals.

A lot of gourmet stores carry excellent oatmeal imported from Ireland or Scotland.

Coarse oatmeal has a distinctively nutlike flavor that goes perfectly with the toasted walnuts in this recipe. The blueberries and heavy cream are ideal complementary toppings.

4 cups water

½ teaspoon salt

1 cup coarse oatmeal

¾ cup shelled walnut pieces

4 tablespoons (½ stick) unsalted butter, cut into about 8 pieces

¼ cup brown sugar

½ cup heavy cream

½ cup fresh blueberries

In a medium saucepan, bring the water and salt to a boil over high heat. Stirring continuously, pour in the oatmeal. Reduce the heat and continue stirring just until the oatmeal begins to thicken, about 5 minutes.

Adjust the heat to a bare simmer and cook about 30 minutes more, stirring occasionally.

Meanwhile, preheat the oven to 400°F. Spread the walnuts on a baking sheet and toast them in the oven for 7 to 10 minutes, just until they begin to darken in color.

When the oatmeal is thick and smooth, with the grains still fairly distinct, stir in the walnut pieces and the butter. As soon as the butter melts, pour the oatmeal into heated bowls. Sprinkle the sugar over each serving, then pour on the cream and scatter the blueberries on top.

Makes 4 servings.

FRUIT & NUT GRANOLA

4 cups quick-cooking rolled oats

½ cup shredded coconut

½ cup slivered almonds

½ cup coarsely chopped cashews

½ cup dark brown sugar

½ teaspoon pure vanilla extract

½ cup toasted wheat germ

½ cup golden raisins

½ cup chopped pitted dates

Preheat the oven to 350°F.

On a large baking sheet, or several small ones, place a separate sheet of foil for each of the first four ingredients. Evenly spread the oats, coconut, almonds, and cashews on their respective pieces of foil and place the baking sheet(s) in the oven. Bake just until each ingredient is toasted golden-brown—about 10 minutes for the oats, about 12 for the coconut, and about 15 for the nuts.

As soon as the oats are done, remove them on their foil, pour them into a large mixing bowl, and, using a wooden spoon, stir them together with the sugar and vanilla. As soon as the coconut and nuts are done, stir each into the oat mixture. Then stir in the wheat germ, raisins, and dates.

Let the mixture cool, then store it in an airtight container at room temperature.

Serve the granola with milk or cream.

Makes about 8 cups or 16 half-cup servings.

MUFFINS, BISCUITS, BREADS & SPREADS

Like well-rounded classical actors, breakfast breads are equally adept at starring center stage or playing a supporting role brilliantly. How many of us, when taking breakfast on the run, happily make do with toast or a bran muffin and coffee? Probably as many as find a breakfast incomplete without a stack of buttered toast or a basket of tender, flaky, fresh-from-the-oven biscuits.

Man, as that old saw goes, cannot live by bread alone. But life—and particularly breakfast—would be a damn sight sorrier without it.

Mark Niederman

YEAST BREADS: A MODERN ADVANTAGE

In our modern age, few of us have the time to bake fresh bread day in and out, and I'm not going to be so high-handed here as to tell you that you have to in order to serve a good breakfast (though you *will* find a recipe here for a good basic toasting loaf, and there's a special, rich brioche recipe in the following chapter). There's certainly no need for you to bake bread, with the incredible variety of fresh-baked breads available today. And I don't mean the presliced, cellophane-wrapped breads many of us grew up with, breads more akin to a kitchen sponge than a home-baked loaf.

In recent years, supermarket shelves seem to have been restocked with real bread: whole loaves kept fresh in plastic bags with twist ties; varied loaves displayed behind glass cases in service bakeries; pumpernickels and rye breads; sourdoughs; raisin breads and cinnamon-swirl loaves; whole wheat and seven-grain breads.

These breads aren't just in the supermarkets, either. In this age of a new awareness of quality foods, ethnic food shops and bakeries are flourishing, and each offers its own range of breads: bagels, crusty Italian peasant loaves, French baguettes, Swedish potato breads, English muffins, and crumpets. All of them are delicious, and all of them are eminently toastable.

One of the best and easiest ways of bringing variety to your breakfast table is to seek out the many different kinds of breads available in your neighborhood. Experiment with them and decide which make the toast that tastes best to you, which go best with your favorite egg dish, which are best on their own or with your favorite topping. Buy a different loaf every week, and you'll never suffer from morning monotony.

FRESH BREAKFAST BREADS IN MINUTES

Every once in a while you *do* want to have something really fresh-baked with breakfast or brunch. That's the beauty of baking powder, a natural mixture of acid and alkaline that, in the presence of moisture and heat, quickly gives off carbon dioxide gas. Mixed into a batter of flour, eggs, milk, fat, and other ingredients, baking powder starts the batter rising as soon as it is added, and completes its rise in the oven—resulting in the quickest of breakfast breads. Starting from scratch, you can have fresh muffins or biscuits ready to serve in well under half an hour.

SPREADING IT ON

Whether leavened with baking powder or yeast, a breakfast bread reaches its fullest glory when adorned with some sort of spread. From butter to peanut butter to cheese spreads, honey to jellies to jams and preserves, breakfasters have a wealth of toppings to choose from. Along with the bread ideas on the following pages, you'll find a number of suggestions for spreading it on, thick or thin, at your morning table.

> *Bread, milk and butter are of venerable antiquity. They taste of the morning of the world.*
>
> —*Leigh Hunt,* **The Seer** *(1840)*

HONEY RAISIN BRAN MUFFINS

The bran muffin is without doubt the classic breakfast muffin—rich and wholesome, healthy and filling. Everyone has a favorite variation; this is mine. The honey gives these muffins a wonderful flavor, and it adds a moist, slightly sticky texture that is irresistible.

Brown raisins are the most common addition to bran muffin batter, but this recipe is graced with golden raisins instead. You could also substitute fresh or frozen blueberries. I've been known to go wild and add walnuts or pecans, and even coarsely chopped candied pineapple or papaya.

2 cups all-purpose flour

½ cup seedless golden raisins

1½ tablespoons baking powder

½ teaspoon salt

1½ cups pure bran cereal

1½–2 cups milk

4 tablespoons (½ stick) unsalted butter, melted

1 egg

½ cup honey, at room temperature

Preheat the oven to 400°F. Lightly grease twelve 2½-inch muffin cups.

In a mixing bowl, stir together the flour, raisins, baking powder, and salt. Put the bran cereal in a separate bowl, and stir it together with 1½ cups of the milk, the butter, and the egg. When the cereal has softened slightly, stir in the honey.

With a fork, gradually stir the flour mixture into the bran mixture; if necessary, stir in enough of the remaining milk to make a thick spoonable batter. Do not overstir: The batter should be somewhat lumpy.

Spoon the batter into the muffin cups. Bake until well risen and lightly browned, about 20 minutes.

Makes 12 muffins.

WHOLE WHEAT BANANA PECAN MUFFINS

We never seem to eat bananas fast enough in our house; there's always one banana left over, its skin almost totally blackened. Fortunately, that's just the sort of banana you need for these tender muffins—soft, overripe, wonderfully sweet.

1 cup whole wheat flour

1 cup all-purpose flour

½ cup coarsely chopped pecans

⅓ cup brown sugar

1 tablespoon baking powder

½ teaspoon salt

1 medium overripe banana, mashed (to equal ½ cup)

1 cup milk

¼ cup vegetable oil

1 teaspoon pure vanilla extract

1 egg

Preheat the oven to 400°F. Lightly grease twelve 2½-inch muffin cups.

In a mixing bowl, stir together the flours, pecans, sugar, baking powder, and salt. In another bowl, stir together the mashed banana, milk, oil, vanilla, and egg. Gradually add the flour mixture to the banana mixture, stirring just long enough to form a lumpy batter.

Spoon the batter into the muffin cups. Bake until well risen and golden, about 20 minutes.

Makes 12 muffins.

MUFFIN TIPS & VARIATIONS

• Most muffin recipes follow the basic proportion of two parts of flour to one of liquid.

• Vary your favorite muffin recipe by substituting buttermilk for the milk; and honey, brown sugar, molasses, or maple syrup for the sugar.

• Instead of, or along with, raisins, try adding other small or coarsely chopped dried or candied fruits such as apricots, apples, cherries, papaya, or pineapple; fresh or frozen blueberries or raspberries; coarsely chopped nuts of your choice; a few tablespoons of wheat germ; crumbled crisp bacon; or even chocolate chips.

• Never overstir a muffin batter; this overdevelops the gluten in the flour, resulting in tough muffins. Stir just long enough to make a slightly lumpy batter.

• If you want a more festive presentation, as well as an easier cleanup, line your muffin cups with paper or foil muffin liners.

• Grease muffin cups with solid vegetable shortening or use a spray-on nonstick coating. Muffin pans with a nonstick surface do not need greasing.

• To test muffins for doneness, insert a toothpick into the center of one; it should come out clean.

Sandra Dos Passos

A GUIDE TO BREAKFAST SPREADS

Keep a good assortment of the following spreads on hand for your breakfast breads.

Unsalted or salted butter (sticks, or whipped for easier spreading)
Plain or flavored cream cheese (block or whipped)
Soft French-style cream cheeses flavored with herbs and garlic (such as Boursin)

Peanut butter (smooth or chunky, salted or unsalted)
Almond butter
Cashew butter
Macadamia butter
Hazelnut-chocolate spread (specifically Nutella, a decadent import popular on European breakfast tables)

Honey (two or more varieties with distinctive flavors, such as orange blossom, clover, coffee, and sage)
Maple syrup
Maple butter (actually a crystallized maple spread that contains no butter)
Molasses
Treacle

Clear jellies (grape is a must)
Lemon curd
Chunky jams and preserves (essentials include strawberry, cherry, and apricot)
Marmalades (a variety, including fine shred, chunky, and mixed fruit)

PARMESAN BISCUITS

I love simple, old-fashioned, American, baking powder biscuits. They're so easy to make, and they turn out so tender and buttery. But I wanted to try something different, and I got this idea from an Italian restaurant that sometimes serves dinner rolls with Parmesan cheese baked right into the dough. The sharp, slightly salty taste of Parmesan is a wonderful addition to biscuits served with your breakfast or brunch eggs.

2 cups all-purpose flour

¼ cup finely grated Parmesan cheese

1 tablespoon baking powder

¼ teaspoon salt

8 tablespoons (1 stick) butter, melted

½ cup milk or buttermilk

Preheat the oven to 400°F.

In a mixing bowl, stir together the flour, Parmesan, baking powder, and salt. With a fork, stir in the butter until the mixture is crumbly, then quickly stir in the milk until a loose ball of dough is formed.

On a floured surface, knead the dough briefly until smooth. Roll it out (or press it out with your hands) to a thickness of about ½ inch. With a floured, 1½-inch cutter, cut out the biscuits, placing them about 1 inch apart on an ungreased baking sheet.

Bake the biscuits until golden, about 15 minutes. Serve hot, split, and spread with butter.

Makes about 2 dozen biscuits.

PERFECT TOAST — THEN & NOW

The next time you're camping, or have flames roaring in the fireplace, try making your toast the old-fashioned way. Cut a thick slice (about ½ inch [1¼ centimeters]) of slightly stale bread and spear it on the end of a toasting fork at least 1 foot long (30 centimeters), so you don't toast your fingers. Hold the bread at least a small distance from the flames (*not* touching them), so its surface evenly faces the heat. Toast until nicely browned, then carefully turn the slice to toast the other side.

The basic principle to follow is: The longer you take to toast the bread (that is, the farther you keep it from the fire), the drier and crispier it will be throughout; the more quickly (and closely) you toast it, the softer it will remain inside. Follow your own tastes.

Modern automated toasters of all descriptions will do all this fine-tuning work for you. Though I own a toaster, I prefer a modern method closer to the old, fire-toasting approach. I place my morning bread under the broiler, adjusting the height of the broiler pan depending on what I'm toasting and what effect I want on that particular morning. It requires sharp attention: broiled toast can burn in a second (but then so can toaster toast). Yet, at that particular time of day, it somehow seems like a more natural approach to cooking.

Brian Leatart

THE PERFECT TOASTING LOAF

We all have in our minds the ideal bread for breakfast toast. For some of us, it's packaged white bread, for others a true San Francisco–style sourdough. Still others may like toast made from rye bread, pumpernickel, or a seven-grain loaf.

I've enjoyed toast made from all those breads and more, but to me the definitive toast is made from a dense-crumbed, fine-textured, white loaf—exactly the sort of bread you'll get from the following instructions. The toast will be even better—crisper and finer in texture—if the bread is slightly stale, two or three days after baking.

8 to 9 cups flour, preferably bread flour

1 tablespoon salt

1 tablespoon (1 package) active dry yeast

¼ teaspoon sugar

3 cups tepid milk (100° to 115°F)

12 tablespoons (1½ sticks) unsalted butter, at room temperature

1 tablespoon cold milk (optional)

½ cup sesame seeds (optional)

In a mixing bowl, sift together 8 cups of the flour and the salt. In a small bowl, stir together the yeast and sugar with ½ cup of the milk; set it aside until the yeast foams, about 15 minutes.

Pour the yeast mixture and the rest of the milk into the flour-salt mixture; add the butter and stir to make a thick, sticky dough.

Flour a work surface with a little of the remaining flour. Empty the dough from the bowl onto the work surface and knead it vigorously until it is smooth, firm, and springy, about 15 minutes, adding more flour a little at a time if necessary.

Lightly oil a large, clean bowl. Gather the dough into a ball and put it in the bowl, turning it until evenly coated with oil. Cover the bowl with plastic wrap and leave the dough to rise at warm room temperature until doubled in bulk, 1½ to 2½ hours, depending on the weather.

Empty the dough onto a lightly floured work surface and push it with your fists a few times to beat the air out. Knead for a few minutes, divide it in half, and place each piece in a greased 8-inch loaf pan. Cover the pans loosely with a kitchen towel and let the loaves rise at warm room temperature until doubled, 45 minutes to 1 hour. (For an even denser bread, use covered loaf pans, fitting on their lids only after the dough has risen in the pans.)

Preheat the oven to 400°F. If you like, brush the loaves, if baking uncovered, with the tablespoon of milk and scatter the sesame seeds on top. Bake the loaves for 45 minutes to 1 hour, until they are evenly golden and sound hollow when turned out of their pans and tapped on the underside with a knuckle. Let them cool on a wire rack to room temperature before serving.

Makes 2 loaves.

> **As to toast, it may fairly be pronounced a contrivance for consuming bread, butter, firing and time.**
>
> **— The Complete Cottage Cookery (1849)**

CINNAMON PECAN TOAST

This old-fashioned favorite is easily toasted under the broiler.

3 tablespoons unsalted butter, softened

3 tablespoons finely chopped pecans

2 tablespoons brown sugar

2 teaspoons ground cinnamon

8 slices white or whole-wheat bread

With a fork, mash together the butter, pecans, sugar, and cinnamon to make a smooth paste.

Toast one side of each slice of bread under the broiler. Turn the slices over and very lightly toast the other sides. Then remove the broiler pan, carefully spread the topping on the toast and continue broiling until the topping is hot and bubbly. Let the topping cool and settle slightly before eating.

Makes 4 servings.

SPICED ORANGE HONEY BUTTER

Honey and butter creamed together make one of the nicest and simplest spreads I know—perfect on toast, muffins, and biscuits.

8 tablespoons (1 stick) unsalted butter, softened

3 tablespoons orange blossom honey, at room temperature

2 tablespoons finely grated orange zest

½ teaspoon ground cinnamon

Pinch each of nutmeg and ground cloves

Put the butter in a small bowl and, with a fork, mash it until creamy. Drizzle in the honey and sprinkle on the zest and spices, then continue creaming the mixture until well blended. Pack into small butter crocks and chill in the refrigerator. Let stand at room temperature for about 15 minutes before serving.

Makes about ¾ cup.

Pooh put the cloth back on the table, and he put a large honey-pot on the cloth, and they sat down to breakfast. And as soon as they sat down, Tigger took a large mouthful of honey . . . and he looked up at the ceiling with his head on one side, and made exploring noises with his tongue, and considering noises, and what-have-we-got-here noises . . . and then he said in a very decided voice:

"Tiggers don't like honey."

"Oh!" said Pooh, and tried to make it sound Sad and Regretful. "I thought they liked everything."

"Everything except honey," said Tigger.

Pooh felt rather pleased about this. . . .

A.A. Milne,
The House at Pooh Corner *(1928)*

ORANGE & WALNUT MARMALADE

The best marmalades, to my taste, are the chunkiest. This recipe gains added texture from pieces of walnut combined with large chunks of orange. It's worth seeking out the bitter Seville oranges to get the authentic bittersweet marmalade flavor.

6 bitter Seville oranges

2 large sweet oranges

2 lemons

2 quarts water

5½ cups sugar

1 cup walnut pieces

Put all the fruit (unpeeled) and the water in a large saucepan. Bring to a boil, then simmer until the fruit is very soft, about 30 minutes. Leave the water in the pan and lift out the fruit with a slotted spoon; set aside. Stir the sugar into the water until dissolved and simmer for 10 minutes.

Meanwhile, carefully cut the fruit into ¼-inch slices, with the peel left on. Remove the seeds and wrap the seeds securely in a small square of cheesecloth. Cut the slices into ¼-inch chunks and return them to the saucepan with the cheesecloth bag of seeds and the walnuts. Simmer for about 25 minutes, stirring occasionally, until thick.

Remove and discard the cheesecloth and seeds, pour the marmalade into sterilized canning jars, and seal. Store in a cool, dark cupboard; refrigerate after opening.

Makes about 6 pints.

FRESH CHUNKY STRAWBERRY SPREAD

When strawberries are at their best, this is a perfect breakfast or brunch spread, quick to prepare and great on toast or muffins. It's not technically a preserve, so store it, covered, in the refrigerator and eat it up within a few days.

4 cups fresh ripe strawberries, stemmed and cut into thick slices

¼ cup sugar

1½ tablespoons orange juice

1 tablespoon lemon juice

½ tablespoon unflavored powdered gelatin

⅓ cup boiling water

In a medium saucepan, bring the strawberries, sugar, and orange and lemon juices to a boil over moderate heat, stirring continuously and crushing the berries. Boil for about 5 minutes, still stirring, then remove from the heat.

Dissolve the gelatin in the boiling water, then stir the water thoroughly into the strawberries. Let the berries cool to room temperature, then transfer to a glass bowl, cover, and refrigerate.

Makes about 2½ cups.

Christopher Bain

MORNING PASTRIES

In one of my favorite Bill Cosby routines, the comic talks about his kids' efforts to convince Mom and Dad that leftover cake is a healthy breakfast food. After all, they explain with wide-eyed innocence, cake has eggs in it, and you eat eggs for breakfast. It has flour, and toast is made of flour. There's milk. And butter. Cake, they logically conclude, is a well-rounded breakfast!

Faulty though that logic may be (except if you're also willing to believe that sugary-sweet cereal makes a decent breakfast), for the legions of people who start their morning with a Danish or a doughnut and coffee, breakfast *is* no more than a piece of cake. And while such a morning meal falls far short of being well rounded, pastries *can* play a delightful morning role—in effect, serving as dessert to a meal that has already included the basic food groups.

Provided you're willing to put in a little effort the night before (an effort you may want to save for the weekend), it's surprisingly easy to make a wide variety of breakfast and brunch pastries. I've simplified things further by reducing everything to just two recipes, on which you can base any number of fancy variations.

Judd Pilossof

· B R I O C H E : B R E A D ·
M E E T S   C A K E

The first of these basics is a recipe for the classic rich French bread known as brioche. Put simply, brioche comes as close as a loaf can come to being cake but still be bread. (In fact, the famous quote falsely attributed to Marie Antoinette—"Let them eat cake"—is more correctly translated "Let them eat brioche.") Brioche is packed with butter and eggs, and you can smell its incredible richness while it bakes, and taste it in every bite.

Brioche is traditionally baked in small or large round fluted pans, but it may be baked in a loaf pan for slicing. Take the basic dough and fill it, twist it, roll it, layer it, or top it, and you'll get fabulous sweet rolls that will put the store-bought variety to shame.

· C R O I S S A N T S : B R E A D ·
M E E T S   P U F F   P A S T R Y

The same goes for the classic French croissant dough—a yeast-leavened bread dough that has been rolled out and layered with butter by the same method used to make puff pastry, resulting in a rich, flaky texture. The recipe here includes instructions for basic crescent-shaped croissants (hence their name). I also like to use the dough as the basis for Danish-style filled pastries, and you'll find plenty of tips for making your own.

B A S I C   B R I O C H E

With a food processor, this dough is incredibly easy to make. It does require some time, though, for rising, and should be started the evening before you plan to bake it.

I've included instructions here for a large, fluted brioche, for twelve individual rolls, and for a brioche loaf. You can also divide the dough into twelve pieces and make them into sweet rolls, following the instructions in the next recipe.

2 teaspoons active dry yeast

3 tablespoons lukewarm (100°–115°F) water

2 tablespoons sugar

4 cups all-purpose flour

12 tablespoons (1½ sticks) unsalted butter, chilled

½ teaspoon salt

6 eggs

1 egg yolk, beaten with 1 tablespoon water

In a small bowl, dissolve the yeast in the water with ½ teaspoon of the sugar. Meanwhile, put the flour, butter, remaining sugar, and salt in a food processor; pulse the machine several times, then process just until the mixture resembles coarse meal. When the yeast has foamed, add it to the processor and pulse the machine briefly to blend it in. Then, with the machine running, break in the 6 eggs, 1 at a time, and continue processing just until a smooth, sticky dough is formed.

Lightly flour a large bowl. Scrape out the dough from the processor into the bowl. Cover with plastic wrap and leave the dough to rise at warm room temperature until it triples in bulk, 3 to 4 hours depending on the weather.

Remove the plastic wrap and punch down the dough. Cover the dough again and put the bowl in the refrigerator, leaving the dough to rise again overnight.

For a large fluted brioche, remove one third of the dough. Shape the remaining two thirds into a ball and put it in a large, buttered brioche mold. With a very sharp knife, cut a deep **X** on its top. Shape the remaining third into a teardrop shape; spread open the **X** and insert the point of the teardrop, to make the traditional brioche topknot. Loosely cover the brioche and let it rise at warm room temperature until doubled, about 2 hours.

Preheat the oven to 400°F. Brush the brioche with the egg yolk glaze and bake until it is golden and sounds hollow when turned out of the mold and rapped on its underside with a knuckle, 45 minutes to 1 hour. (If the brioche seems to be browning too quickly, cover it with a tent of aluminum foil.)

For individual brioches, divide the dough into 12 pieces, then shape each of the 12 portions of dough as you would a large brioche, placing them in buttered, individual-sized brioche pans. Let them rise for about 30 minutes, then glaze and bake until golden, about 20 minutes.

For a brioche loaf, shape the refrigerated dough into a rectangle and place it in a large, generously buttered loaf pan. Let it rise until doubled in bulk, then glaze and bake until it is golden and sounds hollow when turned out of the pan and rapped on the underside, 45 minutes to 1 hour.

Makes 1 large fluted brioche, 12 individual brioches, or 1 brioche loaf.

STRAWBERRY ALMOND ROLLS

1 recipe Basic Brioche dough (page 31), unbaked

8 tablespoons (1 stick) unsalted butter, softened

1 cup strawberry jam

¾ cup thinly sliced almonds

1 cup confectioner's sugar

1 tablespoon hot water

½ teaspoon almond extract

Prepare the dough through its second overnight rising, according to the recipe on page 31.

On a lightly floured surface, roll out the dough into a 12-inch square. Spread the softened butter over the surface of the dough, leaving a 1-inch margin along just one edge. Then carefully spread the jam on top, leaving the same margin, and sprinkle the almonds on top of the jam.

Roll up the dough like a jelly roll, starting at the edge opposite the uncoated margin. Press and pinch the uncoated margin to seal in the filling.

With a very sharp knife, cut the roll into 12 slices and place them on a greased baking sheet. Loosely cover the rolls and let them rise for about 45 minutes.

Preheat the oven to 450°F. Bake the rolls for 15 to 20 minutes, until golden.

Stir together the confectioner's sugar, water, and almond extract. Drizzle this glaze over the hot rolls before serving.

Makes 12 rolls.

SWEET ROLLS: BRIOCHE VARIATIONS

To make fresh breakfast or brunch sweet rolls, prepare a batch of brioche dough the night before and give it its second rising overnight in the refrigerator. The next morning, roll or press out the dough into a square roughly 12 inches on a side. Spread it with a filling, roll it up like a jelly roll, and, with a very sharp knife, cut it into 12 slices.

Or, roll out the dough even thinner—to about a ⅛-inch thickness—and cut it into 6-inch squares. Place a dollop of filling in the center of each square, spread the filling to within ¼ inch of the sides, then fold each corner of the square into the center, press it down, and pat down the fold to hold it in place.

Put the shaped sweet rolls on a greased baking sheet and let them rise for 45 minutes to 1 hour. Bake in a preheated 450°F oven until golden, 15 to 20 minutes depending on size.

After baking, you can glaze the rolls with a simple mixture of 1 cup confectioner's sugar and 1 tablespoon of hot water. For a flavored icing, substitute fruit juice or coffee for the water, or add a drop or two of concentrated flavoring after the liquid has been stirred into the sugar. Then just spoon or drizzle on the glaze.

Here are some filling ideas to get you started:

CINNAMON-RAISIN ROLLS

Mash together 12 tablespoons (1½ sticks) unsalted softened butter with ¾ cup brown sugar and 1 tablespoon ground cinnamon. When creamy, spread over the dough, then scatter with 1 cup of seedless raisins.

HONEY-WALNUT ROLLS

Mash together 8 tablespoons (1 stick) unsalted softened butter with ½ cup honey. Spread it over the dough, then scatter with ¾ cup coarsely chopped walnuts; roll up and slice the dough. Place the rolls tightly side by side in a buttered baking pan and leave to rise. Before baking, stir together another ¾ cup each of walnuts and honey, and spread the mixture on top of the rolls.

SWEET CHEESE ROLLS

With a fork, blend together 8 ounces of ricotta cheese, 1 egg, ½ cup of sugar, 1 tablespoon grated lemon zest, and ½ teaspoon each of pure vanilla and almond extracts. Place a dollop of this filling in the center of each individual square of dough (the cheese may scorch if you prepare this in jelly-roll fashion).

Lynn Karlin

B A S I C   C R O I S S A N T S

Almost every bakery and supermarket around the country now offers excellent fresh-baked croissants for the breakfast table. If you like, though, try baking your own croissants, or use this dough as the basis for filled breakfast pastries.

This recipe takes quite a bit of time, but most of that is waiting for the dough to rise or chill. Still, you're better off saving the project for the weekend, when you're likely to serve breakfast later than on weekdays. You can prepare the basic dough the night before, and the next day you'll have it ready for shaping, filling, and the final rising and baking. From the first rolling out to the baking, those tasks will take about 3½ hours—but you can doze for about 3 of them while the dough does the work on its own.

1 tablespoon (1 package) active dry yeast

1 cup lukewarm milk (100°–115°F)

2½ cups all-purpose flour

2 teaspoons sugar

½ teaspoon salt

½ pound (2 sticks) unsalted butter, softened

1 egg yolk

2 tablespoons water

In a small bowl, dissolve the yeast in a few tablespoons of the milk. Stir in a little of the flour to make a soft, spongy mixture, then cover and leave it to rise at warm room temperature for about 30 minutes.

In a mixing bowl, combine the remaining flour with the sugar and salt. Make a well in the center and add the remaining milk, the yeast sponge,

and 4 tablespoons (½ stick) of the butter. With your fingers, gradually incorporate the dry ingredients into the center to make a dough. Transfer it to a floured work surface and knead until smooth and elastic, about 5 minutes.

Return the dough to a bowl, cover it with plastic wrap, and let it rise at warm room temperature until doubled in bulk, about 2 hours. Punch down the dough in the bowl, cover it again, and put it in the refrigerator to rise again overnight.

The next morning, transfer the dough to a cool, lightly floured work surface. With your hands, pat the dough into a long rectangle about ½ inch thick. Spread the remaining butter evenly over two-thirds of the rectangle's length. Fold the unbuttered third over the buttered middle third; then fold the still-exposed buttered third on top (as if folding a letter). With your fingers, gently seal the edges of the dough.

Turn the dough 90 degrees on the work surface. Dust a rolling pin with flour, and lightly roll it out again to its original rectangular shape. Then fold it into thirds once more, wrap it in plastic wrap, and chill it in the refrigerator for 1 hour.

Unwrap the chilled dough and give it another 90-degree turn, then roll it out and fold it into thirds again. Repeat the chilling, turning, and rolling out process one final time, then rewrap the dough and chill it in the refrigerator for 1 hour more.

Unwrap the dough and roll it out to a large rectangle about ⅛ inch thick. With a pastry cutter, cut the dough into triangles with sides 5 to 6 inches long. Starting at one side, roll up each triangle; as you finish rolling, tuck the opposite point underneath and gently curve the ends inward to form a crescent shape.

Place the croissants about 2 inches apart on a greased baking sheet. Cover them with a kitchen towel and let rise at room temperature for 1 hour.

Preheat the oven to 375°F. Lightly beat together the egg yolk and water and brush the croissants with this glaze. Bake the croissants until golden brown, 15 to 20 minutes.

Makes 12 croissants.

CHOCOLATE CHIP CROISSANTS

While it is possible to sprinkle the chocolate chips on the croissant dough triangles before you roll them up and bake them, you run the risk of chips falling out and scorching on the baking tray. The easy solution is to shape the dough into rectangles, as in this recipe, and seal in the chips.

1 recipe Basic Croissant dough (page 35), unbaked

1½ cups semisweet chocolate chips

1 egg yolk

2 tablespoons water

3 tablespoons granulated sugar

Prepare the croissant dough and roll it out on a lightly floured surface into an 18-by-24-inch rectangle. With a pastry cutter, cut the rectangle into 12 6-inch squares.

Sprinkle the chocolate chips along the center third of each square, stopping about ¼ inch short of the edge on each side. Fold the sides over the filling, and pinch all edges together to seal in the chocolate chips.

Place the rectangles about 2 inches apart on a greased baking sheet. Cover them with a kitchen towel and let them rise at room temperature for about 1 hour.

Preheat the oven to 375°F. Lightly beat together the egg yolk and water and brush the croissants with this glaze. Sprinkle the granulated sugar on top. Bake the croissants until golden brown, 15 to 20 minutes.

Makes 12 croissants.

GARLIC-HERB CROISSANTS

1 recipe Basic Croissant dough (page 35), unbaked

2 medium garlic cloves, peeled

12 tablespoons (1½ sticks) unsalted butter

1 teaspoon dried oregano

1 teaspoon dried rosemary

1 teaspoon dried savory

¼ cup freshly grated Parmesan cheese

1 egg yolk

2 tablespoons water

2 tablespoons coarse salt

Prepare the croissant dough and roll it out on a lightly floured surface into an 18-by-24-inch rectangle. With a pastry cutter, cut the rectangle into 12 6-inch squares.

Put the garlic cloves in a food processor and process until very finely chopped. Add the butter and herbs and process until well blended.

Spread the garlic-herb butter along the center third of each square, stopping about ¼ inch short of the edge on each side. Sprinkle the butter with the Parmesan. Fold the sides over the butter, and pinch all edges together to seal it in.

Place the rectangles about 2 inches apart on a greased baking sheet. Cover them with a kitchen towel and let them rise at room temperature for about 1 hour.

Preheat the oven to 375°F. Lightly beat together the egg yolk and water and brush the croissants with this glaze. Sprinkle the coarse salt on top. Bake the croissants until golden brown, 15 to 20 minutes.

Makes 12 croissants.

FILLED CROISSANTS

The following list offers a good range of other possibilities for croissant fillings. Follow the instructions in the filled croissant recipes on the opposite page, substituting the ingredients suggested below. And use these suggestions as a starting point for thinking up your own variations.

ALMOND-HONEY CROISSANTS

Spread 1 tablespoon of honey inside each croissant and sprinkle 1 tablespoon of thinly sliced almonds over it.

OLIVE & CREAM CHEESE CROISSANTS

For each croissant, blend together 1 tablespoon of softened cream cheese and 1 tablespoon of chopped pitted olives; spread the mixture inside the croissant.

HAM-AND-CHEESE CROISSANTS

Sprinkle shredded sharp Cheddar or Swiss cheese inside each croissant, topping it with ½-inch-wide julienne strips of your favorite ham. If you like an even sharper taste, spread a touch of Dijon-style mustard on the dough before adding the ham and cheese.

JAM CROISSANTS

Place a tablespoon or two of your favorite jam inside each croissant.

WALNUT-CINNAMON-RAISIN CROISSANTS

For each croissant, mash together ½ tablespoon of butter, 1 teaspoon of sugar, and ½ teaspoon of cinnamon; spread it inside each croissant and sprinkle with 1 tablespoon of chopped walnuts and a few seedless raisins.

CHOCOLATE CROISSANTS, FRENCH-STYLE

Break squares or rectangles from a bittersweet chocolate bar and place them in a line across the center of each croissant.

MARZIPAN CROISSANTS

Spread 1 tablespoon of marzipan inside each croissant. If you like, add a spoonful of your favorite jam.

John Dominis/Wheeler Pictures

PANCAKES, WAFFLES & FRENCH TOAST

Maybe it's the conditioning of all those TV commercials I saw for popular brands when I was a kid, but I think of pancakes as the quintessential lumberjack's breakfast. Piled high, glistening with melted butter and dripping with maple syrup (and maybe partnered with a few choice strips of bacon or plump sausages), they seem a delightfully hearty way to fuel up for the hard day's work ahead.

Pancakes, along with waffles, are griddle breads—soda-leavened batters based on flour, eggs, and milk, cooked on a hot greased griddle or skillet or in a waffle iron. While many people see them as no more than a convenient vehicle for syrup, I believe the best pancakes and waffles should have enough flavor—including a hint of sweetness—to be served unadorned. In fact, I'll sometimes eat them absolutely plain—hot, moist, and golden from the griddle or iron, or with just some slices of ripe banana or some fresh berries scattered on top.

Judd Pilossof

· A PANOPLY OF ·
PANCAKES & WAFFLES

Of course, the kind of pancakes and waffles I like in the first place are more than just run-of-the-mill. Among my favorites are earthy, tangy buckwheat cakes; buttermilk pancakes with fresh blueberries; pancakes with bananas cooked right in the batter; whole wheat cakes with pecans; and chewy waffles full of toasted grains and sunflower seeds. You'll find recipes and suggestions here for all these variations and more.

But if it's toppings you're after, as even I sometimes am, I've also included suggestions and guidelines for those who want to indulge.

· FRENCH TOAST ·
LOST BREAD FOUND

French toast is a close cousin to pancakes and waffles—cooked in butter on a griddle or in a skillet, and eaten with butter and syrup or jam. The recipe originated as a canny way to redeem stale bread that would otherwise have been tossed out—hence its French name, *pain perdu* (lost bread).

Good French toast, whether made with stale bread (a wise kitchen economy, to be sure) or fresh, should sit in its egg-and-milk mixture long enough to soak through to its heart, so it will fry up crisp and golden on the outside, moist and custardy within. I've also included instructions for stuffed French toast. And there's a recipe for the Jewish version—*matzo brei*—in which pieces of the traditional unleavened bread of Passover are soaked in egg and fried in butter. It's one of my favorite breakfast or brunch dishes.

PANCAKE & WAFFLE POINTERS

You can use the batters in the recipes that follow for either pancakes or waffles. Yields given in each recipe are for pancakes; the number of waffles you get will vary with the size and shape of your waffle iron.

Add just enough liquid to the batter so that it is pourable and yet still holds its shape in the skillet without spreading to the edge; relative proportions of liquid to water will vary with the type of flour used and humidity conditions.

Let the batter stand for at least 1 hour after mixing. This relaxes the batter and makes it airier, resulting in more tender pancakes. Particularly with pancakes noted for their slightly sour taste—such as buttermilk and buckwheat—resting the batter allows its flavor to develop greater character.

For pancakes, use a heavy griddle or skillet that holds heat well and distributes it evenly. Those made of black steel or cast iron are good.

For waffles, a modern electric waffle iron is recommended, preferably one coated with a nonstick surface for easier removal of the waffles.

Heat the skillet, griddle, or waffle iron moderately hot: a drop of water should bounce on its surface for a few seconds before evaporating.

Grease the cooking surface lightly with butter before pouring on the first portion of batter. From then on, the fat in the batter should keep the pancakes or waffles from sticking. However, if they become difficult to lift, add a little more butter to the cooking surface.

BUTTERMILK PANCAKES

An old-fashioned favorite.

1 cup all-purpose flour

2 teaspoons sugar

1 teaspoon baking powder

½ teaspoon salt

1 cup buttermilk

1 tablespoon unsalted butter, melted

1 egg, lightly beaten

In a mixing bowl, stir together the dry ingredients. Make a well in the center and add the remaining ingredients. Stir, starting at the center and gradually mixing in the dry ingredients to make a smooth batter. Cover the bowl and let it stand at room temperature for 1 hour, or overnight in the refrigerator.

Heat a heavy skillet or griddle and grease it lightly. Transfer the batter to a measuring cup or pitcher with a pouring lip, or use a ladle, and pour the batter into the skillet to make 6- to 7-inch pancakes, cooking only as many at one time as you have room for.

Cook the pancakes until bubbles cover their surface, about 1 minute, then turn them with a wide spatula and cook for 1 minute more.

Makes 12 to 16 pancakes.

WHOLE WHEAT BANANA WALNUT PANCAKES

The mellow, tangy flavor of this buttermilk pancake batter is wonderfully complemented by ripe banana slices and walnut halves.

½ cup whole wheat flour

½ cup all-purpose flour

2 teaspoons brown sugar

1 teaspoon baking powder

½ teaspoon salt

1 cup buttermilk

1 tablespoon unsalted butter, melted

½ teaspoon vanilla extract

1 egg, lightly beaten

3 ripe bananas, cut into ¼-inch slices

¾ cup walnut halves

In a mixing bowl, stir together the dry ingredients. Make a well in the center and add the buttermilk, butter, vanilla, and egg. Stir, starting at the center and gradually mixing in the dry ingredients to make a smooth batter. Cover the bowl and let it stand at room temperature for 1 hour, or overnight in the refrigerator.

Heat a heavy skillet or griddle and grease it lightly. Transfer the batter to a measuring cup or pitcher with a pouring lip, or use a ladle, and pour the batter into the skillet to make 6- to 7-inch pancakes, cooking only as many at one time as you have room for. As soon as the first bubbles begin to appear on the surface of the pancakes, top them generously with banana slices and walnut halves.

Cook the pancakes until bubbles cover their surface and their undersides are nicely browned, about 1 minute, then carefully turn them with a wide spatula and cook for 1 minute more.

Makes 12 to 16 pancakes.

Courtesy The Florida Department of Citrus

BUCKWHEAT PANCAKES WITH CHOPPED HAZELNUTS & MAPLE CREAM

The chopped hazelnuts and touch of molasses in the batter go perfectly with the earthy tang of the buckwheat. Begin the batter the night before, adding the baking soda just before you cook.

The maple cream makes a wonderfully smooth, mellow topping.

1 cup buckwheat flour

½ cup all-purpose flour

½ teaspoon salt

2 cups milk

1 tablespoon molasses

1 teaspoon baking soda

2 tablespoons warm water

1 egg, lightly beaten

2 tablespoons vegetable oil

1 cup chopped toasted hazelnuts

Maple Cream (recipe follows)

The night before serving, stir together the flours and salt in a mixing bowl. Stir in the milk and molasses, then cover the bowl and leave it in the refrigerator overnight.

The next morning, stir the baking soda together with the water until dissolved; stir it into the batter with the egg and vegetable oil.

Heat a heavy skillet or griddle and grease it lightly. Transfer the batter to a measuring cup or pitcher with a pouring lip, or use a ladle, and pour the batter into the skillet to make 6- to 7-inch pancakes, cooking only as many at one time as you have room for. As soon as bubbles begin to appear on the surface, generously scatter the hazelnuts on top of the pancakes.

Cook the pancakes until bubbles cover their surface, about 1 minute, then carefully turn them with a wide spatula and cook for 1 minute more. Serve topped with a dollop of Maple Cream.

Makes about 18 pancakes.

MAPLE CREAM

¾ cup whipping cream

½ cup pure maple syrup

Put the whipping cream in a food processor and process just until it begins to thicken and increase in volume. With the machine running, pour the syrup through the feed tube; continue processing just until the mixture is thick.

Makes about 1¾ cups.

OTHER TOPPINGS

For variety's sake, you might want to have on hand a few alternative pancake or waffle toppings. Choose from:

HONEYS

FRUIT SYRUPS
*(Many commerical brands are available.
Look for syrups with natural flavors.)*

Apricot
Blueberry
Boysenberry
Peach
Raspberry
Strawberry

CANNED FRUITS IN SYRUP OR LIQUEURS
(regular canned fruits or special gourmet products)

Sliced cling peaches
Brandied cherries
Raspberries in kirsch syrup
Raisins in rum

COCONUT SYRUP *(a favorite in Hawaii, available canned in
many large supermarkets or specialty food stores)*

Jerry Howard/Positive Images

SOUR CREAM WHOLE WHEAT PANCAKES (OR WAFFLES)

1 cup whole wheat flour

½ cup all-purpose flour

1 teaspoon baking powder

½ teaspoon salt

1½ cups milk

½ cup sour cream

2 tablespoons unsalted butter, melted

2 tablespoons honey

1 egg, lightly beaten

In a mixing bowl, stir together the dry ingredients. Make a well in the center and add the remaining ingredients. Stir, starting at the center and gradually mixing in the dry ingredients to make a smooth batter. Cover the bowl and let it stand at room temperature for 1 hour, or overnight in the refrigerator.

Heat a heavy skillet or griddle and grease it lightly. Transfer the batter to a measuring cup or pitcher with a pouring lip, or use a ladle, and pour the batter into the skillet to make 6- to 7-inch pancakes, cooking only as many at one time as you have room for.

Cook the pancakes until bubbles cover their surface, about 1 minute, then turn them with a wide spatula and cook for 1 minute more.

Makes about 18 pancakes.

A WORD ON MAPLE SYRUP

The classic topping to pancakes, waffles, and French toast is maple syrup. No other topping comes close to its complexity or mellow flavor.

With every year, however, maple syrup seems to become more expensive and rare. It's no wonder, when you consider what it takes to make just one gallon (3.8 liters) of the syrup. The sap from four mature maple trees must be tapped and collected—forty gallons in all—over a period of a month and a half. Those forty gallons (152 liters) must then be slowly boiled down until only a single gallon (3.8 liters) remains. It's labor-intensive, hands-on work.

But maple syrup is one of those things worth seeking out, a sweet indulgence breakfasters deserve. So-called maple-flavored syrups or pancake syrups are pale imitations indeed.

There are two good grades of maple syrup available. The finest, most expensive, which is often designated fancy, is pale amber in color, with a delicate flavor. Grade A syrups may vary from medium amber in color with a more pronounced flavor (probably a better choice than fancy grade for all but the most delicately flavored dishes) to the rich, darker syrup collected from end-of-season sap—a full-flavored topping suitable for, say, a stack of buckwheat pancakes.

Once you've opened a container of maple syrup, store it covered in the refrigerator. Heat the syrup in a small saucepan over *very* low heat before serving or pour it into a server with a pouring lip and stand the server in an inch or two of gently simmering water to warm the syrup.

PANCAKE & WAFFLE EMBELLISHMENTS

It's easy to add embellishments to your favorite pancake or waffle recipe. Contrary to what you may have done in the past, however, it makes little sense to add solids to the batter: they'll just sink to the bottom of the bowl and you'll find it next to impossible to get them evenly distributed in each serving.

The solution is simple. Mix up a batch of your favorite batter and, right after you pour it into the skillet or onto the griddle, distribute the solid additions on top, letting them sink in while the pancake is still fairly liquid; then flip the pancakes to cook on the other side. For waffles, just scatter them over the batter after you've poured it into the waffle iron.

Here are some suggestions for treats you might like to add to your pancakes. Include them singly or in combination (one of my favorites is bananas and pecans in whole wheat or buckwheat cakes).

FRUITS

Apples (peeled, then very thinly sliced or coarsely grated)
Bananas (cut into slices)
Blueberries
Dates (pitted and coarsely chopped)
Peaches (peeled and very thinly sliced)
Pineapple (cut into thin pieces, or coarsely chopped
and drained of excess juice)
Raisins
Strawberries (ripe but fairly firm, cut into slices)

NUTS

Almonds (slivered or sliced)
Cashews (halved or coarsely chopped)
Hazelnuts (halved if small, or coarsely chopped)
Peanuts (halved or coarsely chopped)
Pecans (halved or coarsely chopped)
Walnuts (halved or coarsely chopped)

OTHER ADDITIONS

Almond macaroons (crumbled)
Chocolate chips (if you like, also stir a tablespoon or two
of sweetened cocoa powder into the batter)
Shredded coconut
Granola
Sunflower seeds
Whole wheat berries

Courtesy The American Egg Board

MATZO BREI

Matzo, Jewish unleavened bread, makes an excellent version of French toast known by the Yiddish term matzo brei. Though it's traditionally eaten during Passover, you'll find it on the menus of most good delicatessens year round—and, fortunately, it's pretty easy to find the matzos to make it with whatever the time of year.

The most common way of making matzo brei is described below, but let me offer you another approach I'm fond of. Break up some matzos by hand into small pieces averaging no more than ¼ inch across. Add just enough beaten egg to bind these crumbs together, and stir in a little powdered cinnamon if you like. Melt butter in a skillet over moderate heat until sizzling, then fry the matzo brei pancake-style until golden brown underneath; flip it and continue frying until done.

4 eggs

¼ cup milk

¼ teaspoon salt

4 matzos

2 tablespoons unsalted butter

In a mixing bowl, lightly beat together the eggs, milk, and salt. Break the matzos into the bowl in rough pieces 1 to 2 inches across. Stir with a fork and let them sit in the egg mixture for anywhere from a few seconds to a few minutes, depending on how crisp or soft you'd like the finished dish.

Melt the butter in a medium skillet over moderate heat. When the butter sizzles, add the matzo brei mixture and cook, stirring frequently, until the egg sets and the matzo brei begins to turn golden, 2 to 3 minutes.

Serve with sour cream, and applesauce or strawberry jam.

Makes 2 to 4 servings.

FRESH RASPBERRY SAUCE

Make this simple fresh fruit sauce in the summer when raspberries are abundantly in season and lowest in price. You can substitute other berries such as strawberries, blackberries, or blueberries.

2 cups fresh raspberries

1 cup sugar

1 teaspoon lemon juice

Put the raspberries in a food processor and purée them. Press the purée through the finest sieve you have to remove all the seeds.

Transfer the sieved purée to a small saucepan and stir in about half of the sugar. Put the pan over low to moderate heat and stir until the sugar dissolves and the sauce is hot. Stir in the lemon juice and add enough of the remaining sugar to sweeten the hot sauce to taste.

Makes 1 to 1½ cups.

Brian Leatart

STUFFED SOURDOUGH FRENCH TOAST

For an extra-special breakfast or brunch, make thick slices of French toast stuffed with a favorite filling. One of the combinations I like best is chunky peanut butter, sliced bananas, and crumbled crisp bacon. (Other filling suggestions follow.) Serve stuffed French toast with maple syrup or jam.

4 (1½-inch-thick) slices sourdough loaf
½ cup chunky-style peanut butter, at room temperature
2 ripe bananas, peeled and cut into ¼-inch slices
4 strips bacon, fried until crisp, drained and crumbled
4 eggs
¾ cup milk
½ teaspoon salt
4 to 6 tablespoons (½ to ¾ stick) melted butter
2 tablespoons powdered sugar

Cut each slice of bread diagonally into 2 triangles, leaving the crusts on. With a small, sharp knife, cut a pocket in each triangle in its long edge, slicing parallel to the sides and taking care not to cut through to the crust.

With a teaspoon, carefully spoon the peanut butter into each pocket, spreading it evenly with the back of the spoon. With your fingers, insert banana slices and bacon into the pockets.

In a large, shallow bowl or dish, beat together the eggs, milk and salt just until the eggs are broken up. Add the stuffed bread triangles, turning them to coat evenly. Let them soak for at least 5 minutes.

In a medium-sized heavy skillet, heat 2 tablespoons of the butter over moderate heat until it sizzles. Add only as much of the bread as will fit comfortably in the skillet and fry until golden brown, 1 to 2 minutes per side. As the egg-soaked bread cooks, it will seal the filling in. Add more butter as necessary as you cook more stuffed French toast.

Sprinkle generously with powdered sugar before serving.

Makes 2 servings.

Sandra Dos Passos

FRENCH TOAST VARIATIONS

There are endless variations on plain or stuffed French toast.

Begin with the bread. It's up to you whether you use white bread, sourdough, egg bread, pumpernickel, rye bread, raisin bread, walnut bread, cinnamon swirl bread, banana bread ... whatever. (My all-time favorite French toast is made with the Italian fruit bread, *panettone*.)

Then slice it and shape it as you like, but not too thin: The bread should be at least ½ inch (1¼ centimeters) thick, and I've had some French toast as thick as 1½ inches (3¾ centimeters). Trim the crusts if you like. Cut each slice into triangles or squares, leave them whole, or use a decorative cookie cutter to cut the bread into hearts, dolls, animals ... you name it.

Then prepare the egg-and-milk mixture, adding any flavorings or enrichments you like: some cream in place of the milk, for example, will give you a richer dish; a few drops of vanilla or almond extract, or some orange flower water, or a dash of cinnamon, or grated orange or lemon zest, add interesting new tastes; a spoonful or two of honey, maple syrup, or sugar give sweeter results. Soak the bread in the mixture long enough to moisten it to its center (the time will vary with the bread's freshness and with how thick you've sliced it).

Once the French toast has been fried in butter, you have the added options of what you top it with. You can just dust it with confectioner's sugar, or a mixture of granulated sugar and cinnamon. Add a dollop of your favorite jam, or drench it with syrup. You can also accompany it with a dish of warm fruit compote (see page 16).

There's a bonus to French toast that most people ignore, but that my father never did. If there's any of the egg-and-milk mixture left in the dish after the bread has soaked, cook it in a little butter after the toast is done, and you have a small side dish of scrambled egg.

Then, of course, there are the stuffing options. Choose from among the following, or add your own favorites:

Courtesy The Florida Department of Citrus

FILLING SUGGESTIONS

Cream cheese and jam (strawberry jam or marmalade are good choices)

Sweetened ricotta cheese with cinnamon

Shredded Cheddar or Swiss cheese and chopped ham

Mashed banana and chopped peanuts

Peanut butter and crisp crumbled bacon

Fresh whole blueberries or sliced strawberries

Chocolate chips

Seedless raisins plumped up in brandy or rum

EGGS

"He was an old buster who, a few years later, came down to breakfast one morning, lifted the first cover he saw, said 'Eggs! Eggs! Eggs! Damn all eggs' in an overwrought sort of voice and instantly legged it for France, never to return to the bosom of his family," P.G. Wodehouse wrote in *Carry On, Jeeves!* in 1925.

It would take a lot of aggravation to make *any* person call down damnation upon all eggs. No single ingredient is more closely associated with the breakfast table or exhibits greater versatility there. Cooked whole by boiling, poaching, or frying; scrambled; made into omelets with myriad fillings and variations; combined with breads, meats, vegetables, cheeses, and sauces in all sorts of elegant presentations—eggs offer something to delight (almost) every palate, from the most finicky to the most jaded.

The following pages survey the many ways of cooking and serving eggs for breakfast or brunch. The intention is to inform and inspire you rather than merely to offer a collection of recipes. There are guidelines for the basic methods of preparing eggs; for making perfect omelets, whether folded or flat; and for preparing soufflés. You'll also find plenty of suggestions and recipes for special scrambles, omelet fillings, soufflé variations, and elaborate egg dishes starting with the classic Eggs Benedict and ending wherever your imagination takes you.

Courtesy Carnation Foodservice

BAKED EGGS WITH SPINACH & CHEDDAR

Baking eggs in small ceramic soufflé dishes or ramekins achieves an effect similar to coddling.

1 large bunch spinach, washed and stemmed

8 tablespoons (1 stick) unsalted butter, softened

Salt and freshly ground black pepper

8 eggs

¼ cup heavy cream

¼ cup grated sharp cheddar cheese

Bring a large saucepan of lightly salted water to a boil. Throw in the spinach leaves and parboil them for about 30 seconds. Drain well and rinse with cold running water. Then gather the spinach together with your hands and squeeze out as much liquid from it as possible. Discard the liquid.

Preheat the oven to 375°F and bring a tea kettle or saucepan of water to a boil.

Butter 4 (1-cup) ramekins or souffle dishes, using 1 tablespoon of butter in each. Coarsely chop the spinach and distribute it among the 4 cups. Season to taste with salt and pepper. Carefully break 2 eggs into each ramekin, keeping the yolks intact. Drizzle the cream over the eggs, and sprinkle with the cheese.

Place the ramekins in a baking pan and pour enough boiling water into the pan to come half way up the ramekins' sides. Bake just until the egg whites are set, about 10 minutes.

Makes 4 servings.

BOILED EGGS

A soft-boiled egg is one of the most comforting of breakfast foods, an egg dish beloved of toddlers and anyone who feels in need of tender care in the morning. Nested in its egg cup, the top of the shell carefully lifted away (by tapping all around it with the edge of a knife or spoon, or cutting it off with one of those ingenious scissorlike devices designed specifically for the purpose and available in most kitchen stores), the lusciously soft-textured white and yolk require just a touch of salt and pepper before being spooned out. Add some buttered toast (cut into fingers, perhaps, for dipping into the yolk), juice, and a cup of tea (coffee lacks the requisite gentleness) to complete a meal that eases one into the day.

To make a soft-boiled egg with the white just set and the yolk liquid, ease the unshelled egg, preferably at room temperature, into a pan of boiling water and cook it about 3 minutes for a medium egg.

Alternatively, you can put the egg in a pan of cold water and then place the pan over moderate-to-high heat. When the water comes to a full boil, cook about 1 minute longer and the egg will be ready to eat.

POACHED EGGS

A poached egg, its compact solid white surrounding a still-liquid yolk, is a preparation of classic simplicity. Perched on a slice of buttered toast or an English muffin, it makes a truly elegant breakfast dish.

Many cooks regard the poaching of eggs as one of the most impossible kitchen tasks to perform correctly, with vivid memories of watching with horror as the egg they've just broken into simmering water disintegrates and whirls about the pan. But there's one essential element to poaching eggs that is all too often ignored: *the eggs must be absolutely fresh.* Only a fresh egg has a white that clings tightly around the yolk; as it grows staler, the white grows looser and the egg becomes harder to poach.

Assuming you have the freshest eggs you can get (which, granted, may not be "farm-fresh"), there are ways to maximize your chances of perfect poaching. Follow these directions.

To poach eggs, put about 1 quart of water with 1 tablespoon of vinegar (which will help the whites to set quickly) and 1 teaspoon of salt into a wide, shallow saucepan. Bring the water to a boil, then reduce the heat to a gentle simmer. One at a time, break each egg into separate small dishes or bowls; then, holding the bowl very near the surface of the water, gently slip in the egg. Add more eggs to the pan, taking care not to crowd them.

Continue simmering until the white is firmly set and the yolk is covered with a slightly opaque film, about 3 minutes. Then use a slotted spoon carefully to remove each egg to a folded kitchen towel to drain. With a small kitchen knife, carefully trim any ragged edges from the whites. If you still have trouble poaching eggs, it's fair to cheat. Buy a special egg-poaching device at your local kitchen store—a metal platform that fits inside a saucepan of simmering water, with recesses into which you break each egg for poaching.

POACHED EGG VARIATIONS

Treat Eggs Benedict and Eggs Neptune as a basic formula and start letting your imagination run wild, keeping the poached eggs as a constant and changing the other ingredients. Try whole wheat English muffins instead of white, or thick slices of sourdough toast; regular bacon instead of Canadian (peameal), or other meats, poultry, or seafood. You can add other flavorings or seasonings to the basic Hollandaise sauce recipe to complement your other variations. Two examples follow.

EGGS DIVAN
Substitute sliced turkey breast for the bacon and place a few parboiled asparagus tips on top before adding the eggs. Stir a little Parmesan cheese and chopped fresh tarragon leaves into the sauce.

EGGS NOVA
Substitute smoked salmon for the bacon. Garnish with a teaspoon of salmon caviar.

EGGS NEPTUNE

Everybody knows Eggs Benedict, the brunch dish featuring poached eggs perched atop slices of Canadian (peameal) bacon on toasted English muffin halves and topped with a rich Hollandaise sauce. In this variation, crab meat is used, and a little orange juice and orange and lemon zest enliven the creamy sauce.

Orange Hollandaise Sauce (recipe follows)

8 fresh eggs

4 tablespoons (½ stick) unsalted butter, softened

1½ cups cooked crab meat, fresh or canned

4 English muffins

Paprika (optional)

4 thin slices orange, cut in halves (optional)

Prepare the Orange Hollandaise Sauce and keep it warm.

Start poaching the eggs, following the instructions given on page 50. While the eggs are poaching, melt 2 tablespoons of the butter in a large skillet over moderate to low heat and sauté the crab meat until heated through.

Split and toast the English muffins and spread their cut sides with the remaining butter. Place 2 muffin halves on each serving plate. Top each half with some crab meat and then a poached egg. Spoon or pour enough Hollandaise over each egg to cover it completely and spread down the side of the muffin onto the plate. If you like, garnish with a dusting of paprika and half an orange slice.

Makes 4 servings.

ORANGE HOLLANDAISE SAUCE

A food processor or electric blender whips up this sauce in no time.

½ pound (2 sticks) unsalted butter, cut into pieces

4 egg yolks

1 tablespoon orange juice

1 teaspoon grated orange zest

½ teaspoon grated lemon zest

½ teaspoon salt

¼ teaspoon dry mustard

⅛ teaspoon cayenne pepper

In a small saucepan, melt the butter over low heat until completely liquid.

Put the remaining ingredients into a food processor or blender and process just until smoothly blended. Then, with the machine running, pour in the melted butter in a slow, steady stream until it is completely mixed in and the sauce is thick.

Transfer the sauce to a small metal or glass bowl and set it inside a larger bowl or pan of hot water to keep it warm.

Makes about 1¼ cups.

FRIED EGGS WITH PARMESAN CREAM SAUCE

I love the contrasts you get in a fried egg—the white firmly set and tasting of good butter or bacon fat, its edges slightly golden and crisped; the yolk thick and runny. It's a wonderfully elemental food, reminiscent of great American all-night diners, perfectly accompanied by a few strips of bacon and some thick toast.

One of my all-time favorite quick breakfasts is fried eggs topped with a simple Parmesan cheese sauce, which follows this basic recipe.

4 tablespoons (½ stick) unsalted butter

1 tablespoon vegetable oil

8 eggs

Parmesan Cream Sauce (recipe follows)

4 teaspoons chopped fresh chives

Put the butter and oil in a large skillet over moderate heat. When the fat is hot, carefully break in as many eggs as will fit comfortably, taking care not to let the yolks break (if you like, break each egg first into a small dish, then slip it into the pan). Fry the eggs until the whites are firmly set, carefully spooning some of the hot fat over the tops of the eggs to help them set more quickly. Keep them warm while you fry the rest.

Place 2 eggs on each heated serving plate. Spoon the Parmesan Cream Sauce on top and garnish with chopped chives.

Makes 4 servings.

PARMESAN CREAM SAUCE

1 tablespoon butter

1 medium shallot, finely chopped

¾ cup heavy cream

¼ cup grated Parmesan cheese

¼ teaspoon salt

¼ teaspoon white pepper

Melt the butter in a medium saucepan over moderate heat. Add the shallot and sauté just until tender, 2 to 3 minutes. Add the cream and raise the heat until it comes to a boil. Simmer briskly until it reduces to about ½ cup, 7 to 10 minutes.

Stir in the Parmesan cheese, salt and pepper. As soon as the cheese has melted and the sauce is bubbly, remove the pan from the heat and keep the sauce warm.

Makes about ¾ cup.

SCRAMBLED EGGS

Did you know that Paul McCartney of the Beatles originally composed the melody for the song "Yesterday" using the words "scrambled eggs"? Trivial, but true.

There's nothing trivial, however, about good scrambled eggs—rich, thick, and creamy. A lot of cooks, though, trivialize the eggs by cooking them too quickly, leaving them tough and dry. The secret behind good scrambled eggs is to cook them over only very gentle heat, stirring them frequently—if not constantly—as they thicken.

You can't be too gentle with them. The best scrambled eggs I've ever tasted were prepared for me and several cookbook-writing colleagues at Time-Life Books in London by the great cook and cookbook writer Richard Olney. Richard cooked them in a small saucepan set inside a larger pan filled with simmering water—an improvised bain-marie. The gentle heat transmitted through the water cooked them very slowly, with Richard stirring virtually nonstop for about thirty minutes. The result was incredibly creamy and rich (he also, it must be admitted, added generous amounts of butter), almost like a custard.

I'm not suggesting you take that long to make scrambled eggs on a workaday morning. But try taking five to ten minutes instead of the usual two or three and see how different the results can be.

To make scrambled eggs, first break the desired number of eggs into a good-sized mixing bowl. If you like, use the edge of an egg shell to remove the white filaments from the clear egg whites. (I do this for aesthetic reasons only, because I don't like their look or consistency.) With a fork, vigorously beat the eggs until the yolks and whites are well combined; stop several times to run the tines of the fork through the more jellylike parts of the whites, lifting them up and letting them run through the tines to break them up.

Melt a generous amount of butter (about 1 tablespoon per 2 eggs on average, but more or less as your taste or diet dictates) over moderate to low heat in a saucepan or small skillet (the eggs will cook more slowly the smaller the bottom surface area of the pan). Add the eggs and cook them, stirring and scraping the bottom and side of the pan frequently with a wooden spoon, until they are thick and creamy. Season to taste with salt and pepper and serve immediately.

EGG POINTERS

• Contrary to popular belief, there is no difference between white and brown eggs apart from the color of their shells.

• Eggs vary in size from small to extra large, ranging in weight (with shell) from about 1½ ounces (46 grams) to 2¼ ounces (70 grams). The recipes that follow are based on medium to large eggs weighing from 1¾ to 2 ounces (54 to 62 grams) each; if you have smaller or larger eggs and are preparing a recipe in significant quantity, you may want to vary the number of eggs accordingly.

• The simplest way to test eggs for freshness is to place them, in their shells, in a large deep bowl filled with warm water. Fresh eggs will sink to the bottom, stale ones will float at the top. If in doubt about the freshness of your eggs, break each one individually into a small bowl or dish before adding it to the other ingredients; your nose will give you all the information you need.

• Store eggs at cool room temperature or in the refrigerator well away from any strong-smelling foods: Their shells are porous and the eggs can easily absorb odors.

Lynn Karlin

CALIFORNIA SCRAMBLE

This variation on scrambled eggs uses ingredients frequently associated with what has come to be known as "California cuisine." Most supermarkets carry fresh salsa in their refrigerated cases.

3 tablespoons unsalted butter

8 eggs, well beaten

½ pound Monterey jack cheese, cut into ½-inch cubes

1 ripe avocado, peeled and cut into ½-inch pieces

6 tablespoons fresh tomato salsa, drained of excess liquid

¼ cup sour cream

4 teaspoons chopped fresh cilantro

Melt the butter in a large skillet over low heat. Add the eggs and cook them, stirring frequently and scraping the bottom of the pan.

When the eggs have thickened but are still fairly loose, add the cubes of cheese. Continue stirring until the eggs have almost reached the desired consistency. Gently stir in the avocado and the drained salsa and continue cooking about 1 minute more.

Spoon the eggs onto heated serving plates and top with dollops of sour cream and the cilantro.

Makes 4 servings.

SCRAMBLES— SCRAMBLED EGGS PLUS

The key to making a good scramble is knowing how to prepare, and when to add, the ingredients. Pick from the list below, or use your own favorite ingredients, and mix them in whatever combinations suit your fancy.

VEGETABLES

Asparagus—cut into 1-inch pieces, parboil, and drain; add 1 minute before the eggs are done.

Avocado—peel and cut into ¼- to ½-inch dice; add to the eggs about 30 seconds before they are done.

Broccoli—cut into small florets, parboil, and drain; add 1 minute before the eggs are done.

Chilies—use canned chilies, or roasted ones, peeled and seeded; coarsely chop or tear into strips and stir in about 30 seconds before the eggs are done.

Mushrooms—slice ¼ inch thick and sauté in butter until all of the liquid evaporates; add 30 seconds before the eggs are done.

Onions—thinly slice or coarsely chop and sauté in butter until golden; add the eggs and cook with the onions in the same pan.

Peppers—cut into ¼- to ½-inch dice or strips and sauté in butter or leave raw; add 1 minute before the eggs are done.

Potatoes—boil until tender, then cut into ¼- to ½-inch dice; add 1 minute before the eggs are done.

Snowpeas—parboil whole; add 1 minute before the eggs are done.

Spinach—wash and dry leaves thoroughly and tear into pieces; add them raw 1 minute before the eggs are done.

Tomatoes—remove any juice and seeds, coarsely chop, and sauté in butter until all of the liquid evaporates; add 30 seconds before the eggs are done.

Watercress—coarsely chop; add raw 1 minute before the eggs are done.

MEATS, POULTRY & SEAFOOD

Bacon & uncooked sausages—broil or pan fry, drain well, and crumble; add about 30 seconds before the eggs are done.

Salamis & other cured meats, poultry & seafood—coarsely chop; if you like, sauté briefly in a little butter; add about 1 minute before the eggs are done.

Fresh meat, poultry & seafood—precook by sautéing or broiling and cut into small pieces or chunks; add about 1 minute before the eggs are done.

Leftovers & cured or smoked meats, poultry, or seafood—cut into small pieces; if you like, sauté briefly in a little butter; add about 1 minute before the eggs are done.

EXTRAS

Sour cream—stir into the eggs at the beginning of cooking.

Nuts (pine nuts, almonds, walnuts, peanuts, pecans, etc.)—toast and coarsely chop, sliver, halve, or leave whole if small; stir into the eggs just before serving.

Fresh herbs (basil, chives, dill, oregano, rosemary, savory, tarragon, thyme, etc.)—strip the leaves from the stems and coarsely chop or shred the herbs; add about 30 seconds before the eggs are done.

CHEESES

Creamy cheeses (cream cheese, fresh goat cheese, garlic herb cheese, etc.)—cut into chunks; add at the beginning of cooking to melt into the eggs.

Dried cheeses (Parmesan, Reggiano, Romano, etc.)—finely grate; add at the beginning of cooking to melt into the eggs.

Hard or stringy cheeses (Cheddar, Swiss, mozzarella, etc.)—cut into ¼- to ½-inch cubes and add 1 to 2 minutes before the eggs are done so the cubes melt partially yet retain their shape; or finely shred and add halfway through cooking to melt into the eggs.

Michael A. Keller/FPG International

HOBO SCRAMBLE

The ingredients may be humble, but the results are delicious.

2 tablespoons vegetable oil

½ pound lean ground beef

3 tablespoons unsalted butter

1 medium onion, finely chopped

8 eggs, well beaten

16 large spinach leaves, washed, stemmed, and cut into ½-inch-wide strips

Salt and black pepper

In a small skillet, heat the oil over moderate heat. Crumble in the ground beef and sauté it until well browned, about 5 minutes, stirring frequently and breaking up the meat with a wooden spoon. Pour off the fat and drain the meat on paper towels.

Melt the butter in a large skillet over moderate to low heat. Add the onion and sauté until it begins to brown, about 5 minutes. Reduce the heat and add the eggs. Cook them, stirring frequently and scraping the bottom of the pan.

When the eggs have almost reached the desired serving consistency, stir in the beef and the spinach. Continue cooking and stirring until the eggs are thick and creamy and the spinach leaves have wilted, 2 to 3 minutes more. Season to taste and spoon the eggs onto heated serving plates.

Makes 4 servings.

OMELETS

There is a definite mystique about the making of an omelet, as if to make one is a supreme gourmet accomplishment. Nonsense! All you need is a decent omelet pan: shallow, with gently sloping sides and a 6- or 7-inch (15- or 17½-centimeter) bottom; made of a good heavy metal that will distribute heat evenly; and well seasoned. To season a new omelet pan, wash it well with soap and hot water, dry it, add half an inch or so of vegetable oil, and leave it over moderate heat until the oil is very hot but not quite smoking. Let the pan cool with the oil in it, pour away the oil, and wipe the pan with paper towels. This provides a fine, natural nonstick surface that you must never wash; just wipe out the pan after each cooking session with salt and some paper towels. (There are also some good omelet pans with nonstick surfaces.)

Beyond that, you just need a touch of know-how and dexterity.

To make an omelet, begin by breaking 2 or 3 eggs into a bowl and beating them lightly as you would for scrambled eggs; season them to taste with salt.

Heat your omelet pan over moderately high heat. Add about 1 tablespoon of butter and immediately swirl it around the pan as it melts. Pour in the eggs at once.

As the eggs begin to set, use a fork gently and carefully to lift and push the eggs from the edge toward the center, letting the still-liquid egg run underneath; take care not to scrape the pan as you do this. Continue the process until the omelet is almost completely set but still somewhat moist at the center.

If you are filling the omelet, distribute the filling evenly across the half of the omelet to the left of the pan's handle. Firmly grasp the handle of the pan with your right hand, give the pan a small but firm shake to get the omelet sliding, and slide it out of the pan onto a warm waiting plate filling-side first; as that half of the omelet comes to rest on the plate, flip the pan over toward the plate to fold the other half of the omelet over the filling.

Serve immediately.

John Deane

"*May I ask you to bring up some herbs from the farm-garden to make a savoury omelette? Sage and thyme, and mint and two onions, and some parsley.*"

—*Beatrix Potter,* **The Tale of Jemima Puddle-Duck** *(1908)*

FINES HERBES OMELET

The "fine herbs" in this recipe are the classic French combination of fresh parsley, chives, tarragon and chervil.

3 eggs

¼ teaspoon salt

1 tablespoon unsalted butter

¾ teaspoon finely chopped fresh parsley

¾ teaspoon finely chopped fresh chives

½ teaspoon finely chopped fresh chervil

¼ teaspoon finely chopped fresh tarragon

Break the eggs into a mixing bowl and beat them lightly. Stir in the salt.

Heat an omelet pan over moderately high heat. Add the butter and immediately swirl it around the pan as it melts; pour in the eggs at once.

As the eggs begin to set, use a fork to carefully lift and push the eggs from the edges toward the center, letting the still-liquid egg run underneath; take care not to scrape the pan as you do so. Continue this process until the omelet is almost completely set but still moist at the center.

Sprinkle the herbs evenly over the still-moist egg. Firmly grasp the handle of the pan, give the pan a small but firm shake to get the omelet sliding, and slip it out of the pan onto a heated serving plate; as half of the omelet comes to rest on the plate, flip the pan over toward the plate to fold the other half over it. Serve immediately.

Makes 1 serving.

MARMALADE' OMELET

3 eggs

½ teaspoon sugar

1 tablespoon unsalted butter

3 tablespoons fine-shred orange marmalade, at
  room temperature

2 teaspoons powdered sugar

1 thin slice orange, cut in half

Break the eggs into a mixing bowl and beat lightly as you would for scrambled eggs. Stir in the sugar.

Heat an omelet pan over moderately high heat. Then add the butter and immediately swirl the pan as it melts. Pour in the eggs at once.

As the eggs begin to set, use a fork to gently and carefully lift and push the eggs from the edges toward the center, letting the still-liquid egg run underneath; take care not to scrape the pan as you do so. Continue until the omelet is almost completely set but still somewhat moist at the center.

Carefully spoon the marmalade onto half of the omelet, and spread it evenly with the back of the spoon. Firmly grasp the handle of the pan, give the pan a small but firm shake to get the omelet sliding, and slip it out of the pan onto a heated serving plate. As half of the omelet comes to rest on the plate, flip the pan over toward the plate to fold the other half over the marmalade. Dust the top of the omelet with powdered sugar, garnish it with the orange slice halves, and serve immediately.

Makes 1 serving.

FRITTATAS

A frittata is simply an omelet served unfolded and in which the filling is mixed with the eggs. Think of it as midway between a scramble and a classic omelet. Though you can cook individual frittatas in a standard-sized omelet pan, more frequently they are cooked in larger pans in quantities to serve several people; slipped out of the pan onto a platter, the frittata is cut into wedges for serving.

While cooking can be done on a stovetop, I find such large frittatas easier to cook in the oven. All you need is a large ovenproof skillet, 10 to 12 inches (25 to 30 centimeters) across.

To make a frittata, beat together 6 eggs and combine them with 2 cups of prepared filling (see the list of ingredients on page 54 for Scrambles). Melt 2 tablespoons of butter in the pan over moderately high heat, swirl the pan to coat it evenly, and add the egg mixture.

Bake the frittata in a preheated 350°F oven until firmly set, about 20 minutes. If you like, sprinkle the top with some grated cheese and brown it quickly under a hot broiler. Use a small knife or a narrow spatula to loosen the edges of the frittata, then slide it onto a heated platter.

Makes 4 servings.

Ed Bock/Manhattan Views

M I X E D   M U S H R O O M
F R I T T A T A

In this frittata, button mushrooms are combined with rich, flavorful dried porcini mushrooms. Porcini are available in gourmet sections, Italian delicatessens, and many supermarkets; they may seem costly, but a few go a very long way.

5 tablespoons (⅝ stick) unsalted butter

1 medium garlic clove, finely chopped

12 ounces button mushrooms, cut into ¼-inch slices

½ teaspoon salt

1 ounce dried porcini mushrooms, soaked in warm water to cover, drained thoroughly, and cut into thin slivers

1 tablespoon chopped fresh parsley

6 eggs, beaten

¼ cup grated Parmesan cheese

Melt 3 tablespoons of the butter in a large skillet over moderate heat. Add the garlic and sauté for about 1 minute. Add the button mushrooms and salt, and sauté until all the liquid from the mushrooms has evaporated and they are nicely browned and completely dry, about 15 minutes. Add the drained porcini and the parsley during the last minute or so of cooking.

Preheat the oven to 350°F.

Combine the eggs with the mushroom mixture. Melt the remaining 2 tablespoons of butter in a 10- or 12-inch (about 25- or 30-centimeter) ovenproof skillet over moderately high heat, swirl the pan to coat it evenly, and add the eggs. Bake the frittata until it is firmly set, about 20 minutes.

Meanwhile, preheat the broiler. When the frittata is done, sprinkle the top with Parmesan and brown it quickly under the broiler.

Use a small knife or a narrow spatula to loosen the edges of the frittata, then slide it onto a heated serving platter. Cut it into 4 wedges and serve.

Makes 4 servings.

MEATS, POULTRY & SEAFOOD

"Elizabeth Tudor her breakfast would make on a pot of strong beer and a pound of beefsteak." So goes an old English ballad. Nowadays, a pot of beer and a beefsteak seem a more appropriate morning meal for a trucker than a queen. But robust dishes of meat, poultry, and seafood still have a secure place at the breakfast table, though they play a more modest role than at other meals.

Sandra Dos Passos

· THE EGG'S ·
ACCUSTOMED PARTNERS

Smoked and cured meats, particularly pork products, are ideal breakfast ingredients. Crisp yet succulent in texture, mellow and slightly sweet in flavor, they complement eggs wonderfully. You don't need a huge serving to enjoy the effect—just two strips of bacon or a pair of sausage links or patties are enough to satisfy. You'll find instructions here on how to cook bacon and sausages to perfection, as well as a basic recipe for preparing your own fresh sausage patties.

There are other options as well. Country ham, thinly sliced and briefly sautéed in butter, makes a fine addition to the breakfast plate. Check your supermarket meat department or your local butcher shop for smoked pork chops, too, which are well worth serving with a pair of fried eggs.

And don't ignore other cured meats. Smoked and cured beef strips, which are cooked just like bacon, are widely available, and fresh lean sausages made from ground turkey can be found with increasing frequency.

· FRESH INGREDIENTS ·

You don't need to consume a one-pound beefsteak to enjoy fresh meat at breakfast. Watch your butcher's case for small, thin steaks cut from the short loin, sirloin, or round portions of beef and weighing no more than about four ounces (110 grams). Sautéed quickly in a little butter and oil, or cooked under a very hot broiler, and served with eggs, they make a breakfast hearty—yet not overwhelmingly so.

The same goes for fresh pork chops. And lean ground beef, shaped into a quarter-pound patty and quickly cooked so it stays moist, provides a healthy portion of protein with which to start the day. I've also had wonderful breakfasts of eggs with a sautéed or grilled half-breast of chicken that has been skinned and boned.

· SEAFOODS FROM ·
THE DELI & BEYOND

Smoked salmon. There's little need to say more than that when it comes to discussing seafood at breakfast. Whether the finest firm, tender, and thinly sliced import from Scotland, or the robust, moist, and thickly sliced product known as nova (for Nova Scotia salmon), smoked salmon (a.k.a. "lox") is the quintessential morning fish.

But there *are* other smoked fish worth trying at breakfast, from cod to whitefish to trout and more. An assortment of these can be turned into a wonderful buffet for weekend breakfasts, for which you'll find a guide on page 63.

While you're at it, check out the fresh seafood at your supermarket or fish store. It's becoming increasingly fashionable to serve fresh seafood at breakfast—particularly thin fillets of meatier fish like salmon and swordfish, which can be sautéed or broiled with a touch of butter and served with eggs like a breakfast steak. It's a thoroughly modern and healthy approach to morning eating.

John Dominis/Wheeler Pictures

SELECTING & COOKING BACON

Bacon is a happy by-product. After the spareribs have been cut from the belly section of pork, what remains is dense, multiple layers of meat, fat, and rind; cured with a brine and smoked, then thinly sliced to reveal the layers in streaky cross-section, these leftovers become the familiar bacon beloved by breakfasters. (Meatier strips of back bacon and rounds of Canadian or peameal bacon are cut from the center loin of the animal.)

· A WIDE VARIETY · OF CHOICES

Bacons vary as widely as the ingredients used to cure and smoke them, tasting of more or less salt, honey or brown sugar or maple syrup, hickory or applewood or mahogany or oak smoke, or any number of other aromatic agents. And that doesn't even begin to touch upon the effect of the pig's diet on the bacon's taste.

Which means to say that you've got a lot of enjoyable taste-testing ahead of you. I've sampled excellent bacon from large commercial manufacturers. I've also tasted exquisite bacon shipped by small dealers who sell their products largely by mail. (And I've had bad bacon—usually markedly inexpensive products on which the makers have stinted as much as possible.)

So check out your supermarket, your local butcher, gourmet shops, and the mail-order ads at the back of cooking magazines. For a large weekend family breakfast, you might want to purchase three or four different kinds and do taste comparisons to see which kinds are the favorites.

Whatever bacon you choose, the meat should have a clear pink or smoky-pink color and a firm texture, and the fat should be clean and white. Store the bacon in the coldest part of the refrigerator, where it will keep for up to a week.

· COOKING BACON ·

You don't need a drop of fat to cook bacon well streaked with fat; provided you start it at low heat, it gives up enough of its own to keep it from sticking. For meatier bacon, grease the skillet with a tablespoon or so of vegetable oil before cooking.

If the bacon has a rind, either cut it off or slit it to prevent it from causing the bacon to curl as it cooks. Place the bacon slices side by side in a large skillet and weight them down with a smaller pan lid to keep them flat.

Place the skillet over low heat and cook the bacon for 2 to 5 minutes per side, depending on thickness, until the strips are well browned and their fat is crisp. Drain well on paper towels.

> *Nothing helps scenery like bacon and eggs.*
> —*Mark Twain* (1890)

HAM & SMOKED PORK

These cured pork products offer an even wider range of choices than bacon, with the additional variation of being either wet-cured—that is, cured in a seasoned brine—or dry-cured with a rub of salt and other seasonings.

Fully dry-cured and smoked country hams need no cooking, and are so firm and intense in flavor that they are best served thinly sliced as a garnish beside eggs, or cut into julienne strips and mixed in scrambles or omelet fillings.

Wet-cured and partially cured hams should be cut into ⅛- to ¼-inch (⅓- to ⅔-centimeter) slices and cooked in a greased skillet like meaty bacon. The same cooking technique should be used for smoked pork chops, which require 5 to 6 minutes of frying per side over moderate heat, depending on thickness.

SMOKED FISH

One of my favorite, most satisfying weekend breakfasts is the smoked fish platter at a local delicatessen. You get a large platter (for two) of smoked cod, halibut, whitefish, and salmon, with lemon wedges, sliced tomatoes, onions, olives, cream cheese, and, of course, toasted bagels.

It's easy to assemble a similar—if not better—platter at home for guests, ordering from the take-out counter and supplementing it with supplies from your supermarket. Make your own selections from the following lists, serving more the grander the occasion, and set them out on individual platters (the fish can share a single large platter) with individual serving plates, knives, and forks.

SMOKED FISH	CHEESES	GARNISHES
Lox (smoked salmon)	Cream cheese	Spanish (purple) onions, thinly sliced
Cod	Whipped cream cheese	Sweet onions (Vidalia or Maui), thinly sliced
Halibut	Flavored cream cheeses with chives or pimientos	Brown-skinned onions, thinly sliced
Mackerel	Garlic-herb cheeses	Pickled onions
Whitefish	Full-cream goat cheeses, plain or with herbs	Tomatoes, cut into slices
Trout	Fresh mozzarella, thinly sliced	Sun-dried tomatoes packed in olive oil
Catfish	Muenster	Fresh chives, chopped
Tuna	Gouda	Fresh parsley, chopped
Sturgeon		Lemons, cut into wedges

Brian Leatart

THE GREAT "SAUSAGE-OFF"

I have the good fortune to live a few blocks away from the famous Farmer's Market in Los Angeles, which includes an excellent stall selling close to a dozen varieties of fresh sausage. There are English-style "bangers" of pork with bread and seasonings, Swedish pork-and-potato sausages, German *bratwurst,* Italian pork sausages either mildly or hotly spiced, and others. Once a month or so, my wife and I visit the stand in preparation for what we call a "sausage-off": we'll buy six or more different kinds of fresh sausage, one of each, and have them for breakfast (or dinner), tasting and comparing the different varieties.

It's a great weekend breakfast idea for a crowd. Hunt around your own city or town and find *your* best source for fresh sausages—be they pork, veal, ham, turkey, or any combination of the above. Cook them up (see instructions that follow), cut them into two-inch (five-centimeter) pieces, and serve them arrayed in a heated baking dish.

• COOKING SAUSAGES •

To cook sausage patties, lightly grease a heavy skillet with vegetable oil. Place the patties in the skillet and place the skillet over moderate heat. Fry the patties for 5 to 7 minutes per side, depending on thickness, until cooked through and nicely browned. Drain well on paper towels.

To cook sausage links ½ inch (1¼ centimeters) thick or less, pierce their casings in a few places with a thin skewer and put them in a heavy skillet large enough to hold them in one layer wihout crowding. Pour enough cold water into the skillet to come about a third of the way up the sausages and place the skillet over moderate heat. As the water comes to a boil, it will draw out fat from the sausages, and when it evaporates, they will begin to fry. Cook them, turning frequently, until evenly browned, 7 to 10 minutes depending on thickness. Drain well on paper towels.

To cook thicker sausages, pierce each one in several places with a thin skewer and place them in a saucepan half filled with cold water. Put the pan over moderately high heat. When the water comes to a full boil, drain the sausages (this precooking ensures that they stay moist). Place the sausages in a lightly greased skillet over moderate heat and fry them, turning frequently, until evenly browned, 7 to 10 minutes. Or brown them under a hot broiler.

Bill Rothschild

COUNTRY-STYLE SAUSAGE PATTIES

Without going to the fuss of trying to grind sausage meat and stuff it into casings, you can make a great breakfast sausage mixture with ready-ground meat shaped into rustic patties. Start with this basic recipe, then try adding your own favorite herbs and spices to vary the mixture. Also, try ground turkey in place of pork.

1 pound ground pork

½ small onion, finely chopped

1 garlic clove, finely chopped (optional)

1½ teaspoons salt

1 teaspoon chopped fresh parsley

1 teaspoon dried thyme, crumbled

½ teaspoon liquid smoke

½ teaspoon freshly ground black pepper

*2 fresh sage leaves, finely chopped, or 1 pinch of
   dried sage*

Vegetable oil, for frying

In a mixing bowl, stir together all the ingredients until thoroughly combined. Moistening your hands with cold water, shape the mixture into 12 patties about ½ inch thick.

In a skillet, heat a little oil over moderate heat and fry the patties until cooked through and golden brown, 4 to 5 minutes per side.

Makes 6 to 8 servings.

ROAST BEEF HASH

1 pound roast beef, cut into ¼-inch dice

*¾ pound potatoes, boiled until tender and cut
   into ¼-inch dice*

2 medium-size onions, finely chopped

1 green bell pepper, seeded and finely chopped

¼ cup heavy cream

2 tablespoons chopped fresh parsley

Salt and freshly ground black pepper to taste

3 tablespoons unsalted butter

1½ tablespoons vegetable oil

In a mixing bowl, stir together all the ingredients but the butter and oil until thoroughly blended.

Heat 2 tablespoons of the butter and 1 tablespoon of the oil in a 10-inch heavy skillet over moderately high heat. Add the hash mixture and use a spatula or the back of a wooden spoon to pack it down firmly in the skillet, on the top and all around its sides, to make a neat, solid cake.

Reduce the heat to low and cook the hash, shaking the skillet occasionally to keep the hash from sticking, until its underside is crusty and well browned, 8 to 10 minutes.

Carefully unmold the hash cake onto a large dinner plate by inverting the plate over the skillet, holding it there firmly and turning the skillet and plate over together. Raise the heat and add the remaining butter and oil to the skillet. Slide the flipped hash cake back into the pan, reduce the heat, and cook it for 8 to 10 minutes more.

Makes 4 servings.

VEGETABLES

I remember the dismay in the voice of a food-writer friend of mine when she told me about the breakfast served to her on her first morning in Tokyo. ''To start off, they brought me a beautiful Japanese bowl,'' she said. ''And inside it was a hunk of iceberg lettuce with soy-and-sesame dressing.''

Though most of us would draw the line at salads, vegetables *do* have a worthy place at breakfast. They play a largely supporting role, however, offering a change of pace to the eggs and breakfast meats, and adding variety to the plate. (A word here, though, on using vegetables solely as a decorative garnish: don't. A sausage patty should not perch on a limp lettuce leaf, nor should bacon strips emerge from a thicket of parsley.)

Favorite breakfast vegetables tend toward the simpler, earthier end of the plant world—potatoes, corn (usually in the form of grits), mushrooms, and tomatoes. Though you'll also find green vegetables like broccoli and asparagus on the breakfast plate, they're commonly tucked inside an omelet; on their own, their distinctive, assertive flavors could overwhelm the more basic tastes your palate craves in the morning.

The following recipes represent classic preparations for the most popular breakfast vegetables. Along the way, of course, there are suggestions to help you take these basics and transform them into your own personal creations.

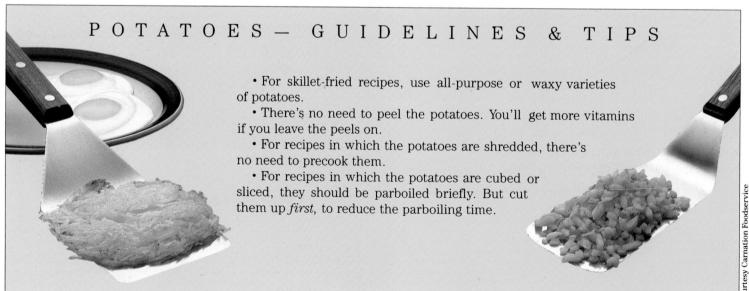

POTATOES — GUIDELINES & TIPS

• For skillet-fried recipes, use all-purpose or waxy varieties of potatoes.

• There's no need to peel the potatoes. You'll get more vitamins if you leave the peels on.

• For recipes in which the potatoes are shredded, there's no need to precook them.

• For recipes in which the potatoes are cubed or sliced, they should be parboiled briefly. But cut them up *first*, to reduce the parboiling time.

Courtesy Carnation Foodservice

HASH BROWN POTATOES GRATINÉE

Classic hash browns as you find them in the finest diners are made from coarsely shredded raw potatoes. The soaking and drying of the shreds called for in this recipe result in good, crisp potatoes.

I've given the hash browns an extra-elegant touch here. Chopped chives are added to the potato mixture and, after cooking, the hash browns are topped with sour cream and Cheddar cheese and quickly finished under the broiler.

1½ pounds potatoes

3 tablespoons unsalted butter

3 tablespoons vegetable oil

½ teaspoon salt

½ teaspoon black pepper

2 tablespoons chopped fresh chives

2 tablespoons sour cream

¼ cup shredded sharp Cheddar cheese

Coarsely shred the potatoes and put them in a large bowl of cold water. Stir the shreds in the water. Then drain them well and refill the bowl with water. Stir, drain, and refill the bowl several times, until the water runs clear. Drain again, then empty the shreds onto a large dry kitchen towel. Rub the shreds in the towel to dry them thoroughly. Preheat the broiler.

In a medium ovenproof skillet over moderate to high heat, melt 2 tablespoons of butter with 2 tablespoons of oil. Toss the potato shreds with the salt, pepper and chives and add them to the skillet, packing them down with the back of a spatula to make a compact round cake.

Fry the cake until its underside is well browned, about 5 minutes. Loosen its edges with a spatula, hold a flat lid firmly on top of the skillet, and carefully invert them together to unmold the hash browns onto the lid. Melt the remaining butter and oil in the skillet and slide the cake back into the skillet to brown on the other side.

Spread the sour cream over the hash browns and distribute the cheese on top. Place the skillet under the broiler until the topping is bubbling and begins to turn golden brown. Serve the hash browns directly from the skillet.

Makes 4 servings.

BAKED POTATO SHELLS FOR SCRAMBLED EGGS

Baked potato shells make attractive, delicious containers for breakfast or brunch egg scrambles.

Use one large baking potato for 2 servings. Rub each potato with a little melted butter or vegetable oil and bake at 400°F until done, about 1 hour. After baking, split and hollow out the potatoes, leaving a ¼-inch shell and reserving the insides for another recipe. (If you like, you can prepare the potatoes to this point the night before, then wrap them in foil and refrigerate.)

Generously butter the shells inside and out, place them on a baking sheet, and bake at 400°F until well browned, about 20 minutes. While they bake, prepare the eggs (page 52) and spoon them into the potato shells straight from the oven.

O'BRIEN POTATOES

This dish of well-seasoned diced potatoes can be elaborated as you like, with crumbled crisp bacon, chopped hot chilies, fresh herbs, diced avocado, shredded sharp cheese. . . . Use this basic recipe as your starting point.

1½ pounds small red or yellow waxy potatoes

3 tablespoons unsalted butter

3 tablespoons vegetable oil

1 large onion, coarsely chopped

1 large red bell pepper, stemmed, seeded, and cut into ½-inch dice

1 large green bell pepper, stemmed, seeded, and cut into ½-inch dice

2 tablespoons chopped fresh parsley

½ teaspoon salt

½ teaspoon freshly ground black pepper

Cut the potatoes into ½-inch dice and parboil them in boiling water for 5 minutes. Drain well.

Heat the butter and oil in a medium skillet over moderate to high heat. Add the potatoes and onion and sauté them, stirring frequently, until they just begin to turn golden, about 4 minutes.

Add the peppers and continue sautéing, stirring and scraping the pan continuously, until the potatoes are well browned, 7 to 10 minutes more. Stir in the parsley, salt, and pepper and serve.

Makes 4 servings.

CHEESE & CHILI GRITS

In country-style diners throughout America, grits are a breakfast staple. Though to the untrained eye they look like a hot breakfast cereal, just waiting for the cream and sugar (and you *can* eat them that way), they are served most frequently in place of potatoes, as a starch, right alongside the eggs and bacon, ham, or sausage.

The basic grits recipe here is dressed up with canned Ortega chilies and mild Cheddar cheese.

3½ cups water

1 teaspoon salt

1 cup quick-cooking grits

½ cup shredded mild Cheddar cheese

2 tablespoons chopped, drained Ortega chilies

2 tablespoons unsalted butter, cut into several pieces

In a medium saucepan, bring 3 cups of the water and the salt to a boil over moderate heat. Stir the remaining ½ cup water into the grits. Stirring continuously, slowly add the grits. Then reduce the heat and simmer gently, stirring frequently, until the grits have thickened to a porridge consistency, about 5 minutes. Add the cheese, chilies and butter, stir until the butter melts, and serve immediately.

Makes 4 servings.

SAUTÉED MUSHROOMS IN SHERRIED CREAM

3 tablespoons unsalted butter

1 pound mushrooms, washed, trimmed, and dried, sliced if large

¼ cup dry sherry

½ cup heavy cream

Salt and freshly ground black pepper

1 tablespoon chopped fresh parsley

Melt the butter in a large skillet over moderate to high heat. When it is sizzling, add the mushrooms and sauté, stirring frequently, until golden brown, 5 to 7 minutes.

Add the sherry and deglaze the skillet, stirring and scraping to dissolve the pan deposits. When all but a thin film of sherry has evaporated, add the cream. Bring it to a boil and simmer briskly until thick, 3 to 5 minutes. Season to taste, sprinkle with parsley, and serve at once.

Makes 4 servings.

MUSHROOMS

Quick, simple cooking—by broiling or sautéing—brings fresh mushrooms to the breakfast plate at their best. When possible, use small button mushrooms with diameters of 1 inch (2½ centimeters) or less, leaving them whole; cut larger mushrooms into ¼-inch (½-centimeter) slices. If you like, cook the mushrooms in bacon fat instead of butter.

PARMESAN-STUFFED TOMATOES

A medium tomato, halved and filled with seasoned breadcrumbs, then baked, makes a terrific morning side dish.

4 firm ripe medium tomatoes

1 small onion, finely chopped

½ cup dry bread crumbs

½ cup grated Parmesan cheese

4 tablespoons (½ stick) unsalted butter, melted

3 tablespoons chopped fresh parsley

2 tablespoons chopped fresh chives

1 teaspoon chopped fresh tarragon

1 teaspoon freshly ground black pepper

Preheat the oven to 350°F.

Cut each tomato in half horizontally. Holding each half with its cut side down, gently squeeze it to remove the juice and seeds.

In a bowl, combine the remaining ingredients. Pack the mixture into the tomato halves, smoothing the tops.

Place the tomatoes in a buttered baking dish and bake them until they are heated through and their tops are golden brown, 15 to 20 minutes. If you like, brown them a bit more under the broiler before serving.

Makes 4 servings.

DAIRY PRODUCTS

Milk and milk products are such common, everyday ingredients that it's easy to ignore them at breakfast time. To many of us, they're just secondary ingredients—the shredded cheese in the omelet, the tablespoon of yogurt in the smoothie, the cream in the porridge—or at most the glass of milk that washes everything down while supplying the necessary calcium ''for strong bones.''

But some of the most satisfying breakfast dishes are dairy dishes. No breakfast is complete in Eastern Europe or Scandinavia without a selection of cheeses to be eaten with slices of hearty rye or pumpernickel bread. I have wonderful memories of breakfasts I ate on Greek islands: fresh yogurt drizzled with the local honey and served with fresh-baked sesame bread and thick black coffee. One of my wife's favorite breakfasts is a dish of creamy large-curd cottage cheese, which she eats with a toasted cheese-and-garlic bagel.

· SIMPLE PLEASURES ·

The beauty of most such dairy dishes is their utter simplicity: just slice them or spoon them onto a serving dish, and breakfast is served. Any well-stocked supermarket or gourmet shop will give you all the variety you require. If you'd like to try your hand at preparing your own special dairy dishes, I've included instructions for making fresh yogurt, along with some ideas for flavorings and toppings.

In addition, you'll find suggestions for elaborating on basic cottage cheese and other creamy morning cheeses. And there are some recipes that take cheese beyond the basics—Welsh Rarebit and Cheese Blintzes.

HOMEMADE YOGURT

Nothing beats the flavor of homemade yogurt. It's easy to make, and you can start it the night before to have it ready by breakfast time. Keep in mind, though, that the yogurt will be at room temperature in the morning. If you want it cold for breakfast, you should start the yogurt going the previous morning, then refrigerate it overnight.

To start the yogurt culture, you will need a few tablespoons of plain commercial yogurt. Choose a brand with a flavor you like. After that, always save a few tablespoons of your homemade yogurt to start the next batch.

(Electric yogurt makers available in kitchen shops do a fine job. If you eat a lot of yogurt, you might want to invest in one.)

Like store-bought yogurts, you can flavor yours however you like: with jam or fresh fruit, vanilla, honey or sugar, lemon or orange zest, sweetened cocoa powder—you name it.

1 quart whole or low-fat milk

2 tablespoons plain yogurt

In a medium saucepan, bring the milk to a boil over moderately low heat, stirring frequently. Remove the pan from the heat and let the milk cool until it registers 115° to 120°F on a cooking thermometer.

Stir the yogurt into the milk, then immediately pour the mixture into a heavy ceramic or glass container with a lid. Cover the container, wrap it in a heavy blanket or several layers of towel, and leave it at warm room temperature for 10 to 12 hours, until it has thickened.

Store the yogurt in its container in the refrigerator and eat it within 3 days.

Makes about 3 cups.

MIXED BERRY YOGURT

Berries are among the most popular embellishments in store-bought yogurt. This recipe uses fresh seasonal berries and homemade yogurt. You can vary the berry mixture as you like, and add more or less sugar to taste.

⅓ cup fresh raspberries

⅓ cup fresh blueberries

⅓ cup fresh strawberries, cut into halves or quarters depending on size

½ cup sugar

3 cups homemade yogurt (see recipe above)

Put the berries into a food processor, reserving a few of each for a decorative garnish, if you like. Add the sugar and pulse the machine until the berries are coarsely chopped.

Add the yogurt and process just until it is blended into the berries. Serve immediately or chill in the refrigerator for at least 1 hour. Serve garnished with the reserved berries.

Makes 4 servings.

Tom Leighton / EWA

COTTAGE CHEESE — PLAIN OR FANCY

Your choices are fairly straightforward here: small or large curd, low-fat or full-cream. Yet there's a surprising range of flavors among the various brands of cottage cheeses—the result of the milk used and the individual manufacturing processes. So it's worth working your way through a small carton of each of the brands available locally to decide which you like best.

Beyond that range of choices, you're also likely to be confronted with cartons of flavored cottage cheeses; mixtures with pineapple or chives are the most common. I find such products insipid. You're much better off stirring your own fresh ingredients into your favorite brand (or into other fresh cheeses such as pot cheese, farmer cheese, ricotta, or hoop cheese). Try the following:

SWEET ADDITIONS
Chopped and drained fresh fruit (pineapple, peaches, apples, kiwis, nectarines, pears)
Chopped dried fruit (raisins, apricots, prunes, dates, etc.)
Jams, jellies, or preserves of your choice

SAVORY ADDITIONS
Fresh herbs (dill, chives, parsley, and chervil)
Dried herbs (dill, chives, oregano, and savory)
Chopped scallions
Ground seasonings (cayenne, paprika, garlic salt, onion salt, mixed seasonings)
Whole spices and seeds (caraway, celery, poppy, sesame, etc.)
Coarsely chopped raw or roasted nuts (peanuts, walnuts, cashews, pecans, etc.)

CHEESE BLINTZES

Serve this Jewish delicatessen favorite with sour cream and preserves (I'm partial to strawberry and cherry). If you like, spoon a dollop of preserves on top of the filling before rolling up each blintz.

Crêpes

½ cup all-purpose flour

1 tablespoon sugar

½ teaspoon baking powder

Pinch of salt

1 large egg

½ cup milk

1 tablespoon unsalted butter, melted

Filling

1 cup cottage cheese

¼ cup farmer cheese

2 tablespoons sugar

½ teaspoon grated lemon zest

½ teaspoon grated orange zest

½ teaspoon pure vanilla extract

1 egg yolk

2 tablespoons unsalted butter

Confectioner's sugar (optional)

For the crêpes, stir together the flour, sugar, baking powder, and salt in a mixing bowl. In a separate bowl, stir together the egg and milk. With a fork, quickly stir the egg mixture into the dry ingredients. Melt the butter in a 5-inch crêpe pan, pour it into the batter, and stir to mix. Set the pan aside, still coated with melted butter.

Heat the pan over moderate heat. Ladle in only enough of the batter to cover the bottom of the pan, swirling the pan to coat it evenly. Cook the crêpe just until its edges turn golden, then remove it with a spatula and flip it cooked side up on a kitchen towel, folding the ends of the towel up over it. Repeat the process with the remaining batter, stacking the crêpes inside the towel.

In a mixing bowl, stir together the ingredients for the filling.

Take a crêpe and place it cooked side up on a work surface. Spoon about 1 tablespoon of the filling across the center of the crêpe. Fold opposite sides over the ends of the filling. Then fold the other 2 sides over to enclose the filling. Repeat with the remaining crêpes and filling.

Melt the 2 tablespoons of butter over moderate heat in a skillet large enough to hold all the blintzes without crowding. When it sizzles, add the blintzes, seams down, and fry them until golden brown, 3 to 4 minutes per side. If you like, sprinkle with confectioner's sugar before serving.

Makes about 10 blintzes, or 4 servings.

Brian Leatart

BASIC BREAKFAST CHEESES

SELECTION

Most people go for milder tastes in the morning, and your selection of breakfast cheeses should reflect such preferences. Choose such semisoft cheeses as Bel Paese, Fontina, Gouda, Havarti, Muenster, and Port-Salut.

If you or your guests like, though, there's nothing against serving a cheese or two with a more assertive character such as a Brie, Cheddar, Gruyère, or even a Gorgonzola or Roquefort.

SERVING

• Thinly pre-slice firm-textured cheeses and cut creamy or crumbly cheeses into small wedges; array the cheeses on a platter.

• Alternatively, place large wedges or blocks of cheese on a large flat platter, board, or marble slab, with sturdy knives or cheese slicers with which guests can serve themselves.

• Accompany cheeses with crusty bread or fresh toast and butter.

• For a Scandinavian- or German-style breakfast, include a platter of sliced cold cuts and a bowl of soft-boiled eggs still in their shells.

• Offer a platter of fresh seasonal fruits cut or separated into individual portions to accompany the cheeses.

Vern Green

WELSH RAREBIT

This old-fashioned British "savoury" is traditionally served at the end of an evening meal in place of dessert, but I find it makes an excellent hearty morning dish. For something more elaborate, pop poached or fried eggs on top of each portion just before serving, or place a couple of strips of crisp bacon or a round of Canadian (or peameal) bacon on each toast slice before you cover it with the cheese and broil it.

1 garlic clove, cut in half

¾ cup beer

1½ cups shredded Cheddar cheese

1 teaspoon Dijon-style whole-grain mustard

1 teaspoon Worcestershire sauce

¼ teaspoon freshly ground black pepper

3 or 4 drops Tabasco sauce

8 slices bread

Preheat the broiler. Rub the bottom of a medium saucepan with the cut sides of the garlic clove. Discard the garlic. Add the beer to the pan and bring it to a boil over moderately high heat.

Remove the pan from the heat, sprinkle in the cheese, and add the seasonings. Stir until the cheese has melted.

Toast the bread. Place 2 slices on each heatproof serving plate (or in shallow oven-to-table baking dishes). Pour the cheese over the toast and broil until bubbly and golden brown, 3 to 5 minutes. Carefully place the plates or dishes on top of larger service plates and serve immediately.

Makes 4 servings.

HOT DRINKS

No matter how enticing the aromas wafting from the kitchen may be, no matter how seductive the fruit or eggs or sausages or pancakes look on the breakfast plate, no matter how cheery the table may be set and the morning may look outside the window, the sluggish mind requires something more.

It is no coincidence, then, that the three most popular hot morning beverages—coffee, tea and chocolate—are all liberally laced with caffeine. Each of these hot drinks combines wonderful aromas and flavors with the reviving benefits of that well-known stimulant.

This is not the place to question whether anyone actually *needs* caffeine. There are excellent decaffeinated coffees available, particularly in whole beans that you grind yourself; the loss of flavor seems, to my tastebuds, minimal, though you definitely miss the ''kick.'' Decaffeinated teas, I find, are somewhat insipid, the decaffeinating process detracting from the tea's more delicate qualities. Decaffeination aside, brewing your tea or coffee correctly can ensure that whatever good flavor it does have will fully emerge.

Judd Pilossof

I turned the hot water on and got the coffee-maker down off the shelf. I wet the rod and measured the stuff into the top and by that time the water was steaming. I filled the lower half of the dingus and set it on the flame. I set the upper part on top and gave it a twist so it would bind.

• • •

The coffee-maker was almost ready to bubble. I turned the flame low and watched the water rise. It hung a little at the bottom of the glass tube. I turned the flame up just enough to get it over the hump and then turned it low again quickly. I stirred the coffee and covered it. I set my timer for three minutes. Very methodical guy, Marlowe. Nothing must interfere with his coffee technique. Not even a gun in the hand of a desperate character.

—Raymond Chandler, **The Long Goodbye**

COFFEE BREWING METHODS

Everyone has his or her favorite way to make morning coffee, and I'm not going to alienate anyone by declaring one method better than another. I've had wonderful coffee made in a ceramic jug and poured through a strainer, carefully dripped through a filter, and percolated over a campfire. (My preferred approach, I'll admit, is the drip method.)

Whatever method you choose, you should, however, follow these basic guidelines to ensure that your coffee tastes its best:

Keep your coffeemaking equipment absolutely clean. The oils in coffee that give it its flavor can leave behind a residue that quickly turns rancid and spoils the taste of future brews. After use, always wash your equipment with hot soapy water, then rinse well.

Use fresh, pure water. The flavor of your water will affect the flavor of your coffee. If you live in an area with water that is heavily chlorinated or otherwise treated, use bottled water. And always start with fresh water; water that has been boiled once, then has been cooled and reboiled again, will taste flat.

Don't use water at a full boil. The fullest flavor is extracted from coffee by water a few degrees below the boiling point. When using the drip or jug methods, let the water sit for about one minute after it boils and before you pour it over the coffee. Take care with percolators that the pot goes over moderate heat, so that it doesn't perk at a full boil.

Use fresh coffee, freshly ground. To preserve its flavor longer, buy your coffee in whole beans and store them in an airtight container in the refrigerator or, preferably, the freezer. Grind the coffee just before you brew it, as fine as you can without clogging your brewing or filtering apparatus.

Don't stint on the coffee. Use two tablespoons of ground coffee to every cup of water as your starting point. Adjust the quantities to suit your taste and your brewing apparatus.

Don't let coffee sit. If you like making coffee in quantity so you can go on serving it throughout the meal, it's worth investing in a thermos pitcher with a screw-on top, available in most kitchenware and coffee stores. Keeping coffee warm over a heat source quickly turns it bitter, giving it the familiar "stewed" flavor you find in bad diners.

• THE JUG METHOD •

Put the ground coffee in a heavy ceramic or earthenware jug and pour the boiled water over it. Stir with a wooden spoon. Let the coffee sit for five minutes, then pour it through a small, fine-mesh strainer into coffee cups.

• THE PLUNGER POT •

In this modern variation on the jug method, the coffee and water are combined in an attractive glass serving jug with straight sides. A lid on top of the jug supports a fine-meshed plunger that tightly hugs the inside of the pot. After five minutes, the plunger is pushed down to trap the coffee grounds on the bottom before pouring.

· THE DRIP METHOD ·

If you have an automatic drip machine, the work is done for you. If, however, you simply have a filter set over a pot, follow these instructions:

Bring fresh water to a boil. Meanwhile, grind the coffee and put it in the filter paper set inside the filter holder.

When the water reaches a boil, pour some directly into the pot and swirl it around to warm the pot. Pour out the water.

Set the filter over the pot. Pour a good splash of water over the coffee—just enough to wet the grounds and cause them to swell, so that the water will drip through more slowly. Then pour in the water to fill the filter by about two-thirds; continue pouring as the filter empties.

· PERCOLATION ·

Open the pot and remove the coffee basket and stem. Rinse them with cold water but do not dry them. Fill the basket with the required amount of coffee. Fill the pot with the corresponding amount of cold water and return the stem and basket to the pot, putting the lid on securely.

For electric pots, just follow directions. For stovetop pots, place the percolator over moderate heat and gently bring the water to a boil. As soon as it begins perking, reduce the heat as much as you can while still allowing percolation to continue. Perk for six to eight minutes, until the coffee has reached the desired strength, then remove the pot from the heat and serve.

The intelligent man who empties these cups of foaming coffee, he alone knows truth.

—old Arabic poem

This coffee plunges into the stomach, and immediately there is overall commotion. The mind is aroused, ideas pour forth like the battalions of the Grande Armée on the field of battle, and the fight begins. Memories charge at full gallop, their banners flying in the wind. The light cavalry of comparisons deploys itself magnificently; the artillery of logic hurry in with their train of ammunition; flashes of wit pop up like sharpshooters. Similes arise and the paper covers with ink: for the struggle commences and concludes with torrents of black liquid, just as a battle with powder.

**—Honoré de Balzac,
Treatise on Modern Stimulants**

COFFEE VARIETIES

The flavor of coffee can vary widely, depending on the kind of coffee tree, the terrain in which it was grown, the weather to which it was subjected, the means by which the beans were harvested and prepared, and how the coffee was roasted.

Go to any coffee store and you'll find anywhere from four or five to as many as two dozen different kinds of coffees, usually named after the country or region in which they were produced. You'll also find coffee blends, combining two or more different kinds of beans with complementary characteristics. (And you'll find, likely as not, a new trend I find rather irksome—coffee beans flavored with chocolate, vanilla, cinnamon, mint and other essences that, to my taste, disguise it rather than improve it.)

Morning coffees, moderately roasted, tend towards milder, fuller flavors with low acidity. But some people, conversely, prefer good strong coffee, dark-roasted, to get them going in the morning. It's simply a matter of taste.

Use the following descriptions as a beginning for your own explorations into the many coffee varieties available:

ANGOLA
A strong, smooth coffee, often used in blends.

ANTIGUA
Sharp, rich, sweet, and aromatic.

BRAZILIAN BOURBON SANTOS
Smooth and sweet, with medium body and high acidity.

CELEBES
Very aromatic, with medium body and rich flavor.

COLOMBIA
Full-bodied, rich, and well-balanced.

COSTA RICA
Excellent aroma, full-bodied, rich, and smooth.

GUATEMALA
Full-bodied, with mellow flavor and aroma.

HAITI
Sweet and rich, with high acidity.

INDIA MYSORE
Good body, light flavor, and low acidity.

JAMAICA
Celebrated for the now-rare Blue Mountain coffee—mellow, rich, highly aromatic, and sweet.

JAVA
Smooth, mild and wonderfully aromatic; most often blended with Mocha.

KENYA
Full-bodied, with a sharp-sweet, slightly winey taste.

KONA
A medium-bodied coffee with a fine aroma and a somewhat nutlike flavor.

MEXICO
Aromatic, mellow-flavored, and full-bodied.

MOCHA
Full-bodied with excellent aroma and almost chocolatey flavor; usually blended with Java.

NEW GUINEA
A medium-bodied coffee with excellent aroma and sweet flavor.

SUMATRA
Heavy-bodied, full-flavored, and sweet.

· A BRIEF WORD ·
ON CREAM & SUGAR

I drink my morning coffee black and unsweet-ened—except when I happen to be in France or Italy, when I take it as *café au lait* or *caffe latte*, an almost fifty-fifty mixture of strong black coffee and hot milk.

There's no definitive word to give on how you should take your morning coffee; a drop or more of cream if you like the rich smoothness it adds (a great way to take the edge off a more acidic or darkly roasted brew); milk if you like, perhaps heated first if you don't want it to cool down the coffee; sugar, or sugar substitute; or brown sugar, raw sugar or honey if you picture yourself as living in touch with nature.

But let me offer one edict: Never, never, never use powdered or liquid artificial milk or cream substitutes (you know their familiar names with-out my naming them). In the interest of science, I once tasted one right out of the carton; at best it reminded me of milk of magnesia, at worst.... While they seem to enrich and smooth coffee, I find they give a strange chemical aftertaste. Don't insult good coffee.

I turned on the pillow with a little moan, and at this juncture Jeeves entered with the vital oolong. I clutched at it like a drown-ing man at a straw hat. A deep sip or two, and I felt—I won't say restored, because a birthday party like Pongo Twistleton's isn't a thing you get restored after with a mere mouthful of tea, but sufficiently the old Bertram to be able to bend the mind on this awful thing which had come upon me.

—*P.G. Wodehouse*, **Right Ho, Jeeves**

A GUIDE TO
MORNING TEAS

Without going into a thorough discussion of the botany, cultivation, and processing of *Camellia sinensis*, the flowering evergreen whose dried leaves are known as tea, suffice it to say that there are dozens of different varieties to choose from—delicate or strong-flavored, unblended or blended, pure or combined with exotic flavors and scents.

While you can drink any tea of your choosing at breakfast, some are generally accepted as being more suited than others to early morning con-sumption. Generally, the "black" teas such as Assam, Ceylon, Darjeeling, Keemun and Orange Pekoe have the richness and body to make a sustaining morning drink, and to stand up well to the milk often added to breakfast tea (though lemon is also an acceptable addition); lighter "oolong" teas are also good in the morning; deli-cate "green" teas are more appropriate at other times of day.

In addition, certain teas are specifically blended for morning consumption. Among the best-known:

English Breakfast. A blend of Indian and Ceylonese black teas, strong in the cup yet smooth and somewhat sweet. Add milk and sugar to taste.

French Blend. Largely Chinese black tea, with a little Indian or Ceylonese added for extra body and flavor. Serve with milk and sugar.

Irish Breakfast Tea. A robust blend of Assam and Ceylonese black teas, served with milk and sugar.

You might also like to try one of these flavored teas:

Cinnamon Tea. Ground cinnamon combined with a blend of black teas. You can also make your own by breaking a cinnamon stick into the teapot before brewing.

Earl Grey. A popular commercial blend flavored with oil of bergamot. Serve with milk or lemon.

Lemon or Orange Tea. Tea blended with dried lemon or orange rind. If you like, strip the colored zest from an orange or lemon and add it to the pot before brewing.

Mint Tea. Tea blended with dried peppermint or spearmint leaves. If you like, add fresh or dried mint leaves to the pot yourself.

· HERB TEAS ·

Herb tea can be a delightful change of pace for those who want to cut down on or eliminate caffeine from their morning beverage. Use any of the following ingredients, singly or blended in any combination that is pleasing to you, with or without regular tea added to taste. If you like, add some broken cinnamon, shredded orange or lemon zests, a little fresh chopped or dried powdered ginger, powdered cloves, or grated nutmeg to spice up the tea.

Allow one teaspoon of dried ingredients per cup, and let the herbs steep for ten to fifteen minutes, according to taste, before pouring.

Chamomile. A gentle, sweet-scented, and soothing tea.

Cinnamon. Spicy and sweet.

Lemon Grass. A sharp, citrusy aroma and taste.

Lemon Verbena. Though unrelated to lemon grass, an equally citrusy drink.

Mint. Refreshing, bracing, and naturally sweet. Choose from spearmint or peppermint.

Rose Hips. Sweet, sharp, and tangy; high in vitamin C.

SIMPLE STEPS TO PERFECT TEA

1. Fill a kettle or pot with fresh, cold water and bring it to a boil over high heat.

2. Meanwhile, run the hot water tap and, when it is running as hot as possible, fill the teapot with hot water.

3. As soon as the kettle is boiling, empty the teapot and add one teaspoon of tea to the pot for each cup. For six or more cups, add one extra teaspoon. (Some modern teapots have an infuser insert into which the tea is spooned; after brewing, the infuser can be lifted out to prevent the tea in the pot from getting stronger.)

4. Pour the water from the kettle over the tea and replace the lid.

5. Let the tea steep for four to five minutes, depending on desired strength. Remove the infuser if necessary. If the tea is loose in the pot, pour the tea through a strainer. Keep the pot warm by covering it with a tea cozy.

Lynn Karlin

A BASIC CUP OF COCOA

You can't go wrong with these basic directions. The better the quality of the cocoa you start with, the better the final results.

2 heaping tablespoons unsweetened cocoa

2 heaping tablespoons sugar

½ cup hot water

3½ cups milk

In a saucepan, combine the cocoa and sugar. Stir in the hot water and place the pan over moderate heat, stirring continuously until the mixture begins to bubble.

Immediately stir in the milk and continue stirring until the milk is hot but not yet boiling.

Remove the pan from the heat and, with a wire whisk or an egg beater, beat the cocoa for 15 seconds, until it is smooth and frothy. Pour it immediately into mugs.

Makes 4 servings.

When you have breakfasted well and full, if you will drink a big cup of chocolate at the end you will have digested the whole perfectly three hours later, and you will still be able to dine. . . . Because of my scientific enthusiasm and the sheer force of my eloquence I have persuaded a number of ladies to try this, although they were convinced it would kill them; they have always found themselves in fine shape indeed, and have not forgotten to give the Professor his rightful due.

People who habitually drink chocolate enjoy unvarying health, and are least attacked by a host of little illnesses which can destroy the true joy of living; their physical weight is almost stationary: these are two advantages which anyone can verify among his acquaintanceship and especially among his friends who follow this diet.

—Jean Anthelme Brillat-Savarin,
The Physiology of Taste
(translated by M.F.K. Fisher)

SECTION II:
TABLE SETTINGS

John Deane

TABLE SETTINGS

As much as—and sometimes even more than—the foods you serve, the style in which you present breakfast creates a mood that sets the tone for the entire day. A bountiful weekend brunch table covered with an antique lace or linen cloth and topped with country pottery, bone-handled cutlery, a napkin-lined muffin basket, stout pitchers for milk or juice, an earthenware vase of wildflowers, delivers an elemental message: Here is nourishment, sustenance amidst comfort, beauty and simplicity. Life is *good*, it says. Even the table you set for a hasty weekday breakfast snatched as you rush off to work can help hone your winning edge: china and stainless steel cutlery, bold-patterned napkins, and a bud vase with a single flower take less than a minute to set out on the kitchen counter; yet they can help inspire a confident quest for excellence.

It isn't necessary to spend a lot of time or money on your table settings. Imagination—coupled with a touch of planning—is the key.

Try setting the breakfast table the night before. Perform it as the last task after clearing away the dinner dishes, and you'll hardly notice you've done it.

You don't need much in the way of special breakfast or brunch tableware, either. Just select from your household collection of dishes—no matter how limited it may be—and bear in mind the foods you'll be serving and any particular mood you might want to establish. Even the humblest dishes, set out with care and with a few inexpensive touches that show the thought you've put into the meal, will make your breakfast a special one.

On the following pages, you'll find general guidelines and specific suggestions to spark your imagination. If you have fun setting your breakfast table, that sense of fun cannot help but carry over into the rest of the day.

James R. Levin/FPG International

H O W   T H E   B R E A K F A S T   T A B L E   I S   S E T

Most mornings, you'll want to keep the table simple. Likely as not, you'll be sitting in the kitchen, the hub of most homes, at the table or counter. On weekdays you probably won't be eating too elaborate a meal. You may just need one dish: a dinner plate if you're having eggs or pancakes; a bowl if it's cereal or yogurt or fruit salad; or just a small bread plate for muffins, croissants, toast or rolls. Add appropriate cutlery, juice glasses, and mugs or cups and saucers, and the setting is complete.

The table for an elaborate breakfast, whether served in the kitchen, dining room, or wherever the breakfasters are assembling, may call for all these items and more. Whatever kind of breakfast or brunch you serve, here are the general categories to consider for each place setting:

· B O W L S ·

For hot or cold cereals, fruit salads, or yogurt, you need standard-sized, deep individual bowls, about six inches (fifteen centimeters) across at the top; these are also good for holding grapefruit or cantaloupe halves. If you like, you can use wide, shallow soup plates instead; they make it easier to spoon up cereals and finely diced fruits (though their greater surface area lets hot cereals cool down more quickly).

Courtesy The Florida Department of Citrus

· DINNER PLATES ·

For eggs, pancakes, French toast, hashes, or other main course dishes, ten-inch (twenty-five-centimeter) luncheon plates do fine. But for a really large, buffet-style breakfast or brunch, your guests may welcome the additional space of a twelve-inch (thirty-centimeter) dinner plate.

Brian Leatart

Brian Leatart

· BREAD PLATES ·

Use six- or eight-inch (fifteen- or twenty-centimeter) bread or salad plates to hold muffins, toast, bagels, sweetrolls, or other breakfast breads. For informal morning meals, though, you can dispense with these and serve the bread right on the main plate.

· SPECIAL DISHES ·

Some individual servings of breakfast or brunch foods are best served in special dishes. For soft-boiled eggs, egg cups are ideal; you can buy inexpensive pottery varieties in most kitchen stores, or, like a friend once did, you can start a collection of souvenir egg cups that you buy on your travels. Avocado-shaped bowls meant for serving avocado halves at lunch or dinner are ideal for holding halves of fresh papaya, or any sliced fruits or fruit salads. Keep an eye out for other specialized dishes that can do their duty at breakfast—small bowls to hold poached eggs, for example, or individual gratin dishes to hold servings of broiled tomatoes, mushrooms, or Welsh rarebits.

Sandra Dos Passos

· GLASSES ·

For milk and juices, have sturdy, straight-sided glasses that hold generous servings—six to eight ounces (180 to 240 milliliters) or more. Clear glass lets the natural color of the beverage shine through. Have smaller glasses on hand, as well, for those who don't like to chug down large servings of juice.

· CUPS & MUGS ·

For tea, coffee or cocoa, you can use a standard set of cups and saucers. Mugs hold larger servings of hot drinks and, being generally heavier than cups, keep them hotter longer. They're ideal for everyday use or for informal breakfasts.

· CUTLERY ·

For a full breakfast or brunch, you'll need the standard cutlery: a large fork for the main course; a smaller fork for fruit salads; a knife; a smaller butter knife; a large spoon for cereal or fruits; a smaller spoon for stirring hot drinks.

Fred Lyon/Wheeler Pictures

THE INDIVIDUAL PLACE SETTING

Arrange the breakfast or brunch place setting as you would a setting for lunch or dinner. At the center, place the main luncheon- or dinner-sized plate (or a fruit or cereal bowl, or a bread plate, if that's all you're serving). On top of the main plate, place a bowl if you're starting with cereal, fruit salad or yogurt; it will be removed before the main course is served. Put a side plate for bread above and to the left of the main plate.

Put the fork to the left of the main plate, and the knife to the right. If you have a butter knife, rest it across the topmost rim of the bread plate. Place cereal spoons on the far right of the setting, or above the top of the main plate. At the top-right corner of the setting, place the juice glass, and cup and saucer or mug. You can place the napkin beneath the fork, or to its left, or even on top of the main plate.

Lynn Karlin

PLATTERS & SERVING DISHES

While most of us pay *some* attention to the dishes we eat our breakfast on, few of us give much thought to what we serve our breakfasts *from*. The skillet in which you've cooked your eggs, corned beef hash, or O'Brien potatoes is often the best serving dish for them, placed on the table atop a heatproof pad. But how many of us grab the first battered skillet that we see? For a more appealing meal, be sure to choose your most attractive cooking vessel—perhaps a gleaming copper pan, or a heavy black cast-iron skillet. The more eye-catching the utensil you cook in and serve from, the better your breakfast foods will look.

If you're serving breakfast or brunch to a crowd, a collection of heatproof serving platters and covered dishes or casseroles is invaluable. Keep them warm in a low oven for holding bacon, pancakes, or other dishes that you cook in several batches; then transfer them to the table when the meal is ready to serve.

Use large platters for presenting cold cuts, cheeses, or smoked fish, or for arraying fresh fruit. Large bowls come in handy for fruit salads. Chill them before use.

Lined with a heavy napkin or kitchen towel, bowls are also handy for holding fresh-baked breads or hot toast: Fold the corners of the napkin over the breads to keep them warm. Small country-style baskets are an attractive alternative for this purpose.

Use small bowls or serving dishes to hold whipped cream cheeses, jams, preserves, or sauces. Small pitchers are needed for cream, milk, or syrups. Use a large pitcher for milk or juices.

Don't forget serving trays, particularly for that most delightful of morning meals: *breakfast in bed*. It's good to have a pair of individual trays, with or without legs that support them over the lap in bed, and to have a larger tray for transporting food, coffee pots, baskets of breads and so on. Such trays are also convenient for carrying food for a large breakfast from the kitchen to the table, and they make clearing away the breakfast dishes much easier.

THE BREAKFAST & BRUNCH ENVIRONMENT

Your table covering, napkins, placemats, and centerpieces or decorations complete the mood of the breakfast table. Taking a few extra moments to consider such grace notes can help elevate any breakfast to the rank of a truly memorable meal.

· TABLE TOPS ·

Since the all-purpose kitchen table is the most common site for everyday morning meals, more breakfasts are probably eaten on plastic laminated surfaces than on any other type of table top. And with good reason. Most such surfaces are decorated in cheery colors and patterns, and they wipe clean, making fast work of post-meal clearing. Whether your kitchen table or counter has a plastic laminate top or is butcher block or some other surface, it provides an appropriate background for most breakfasts.

But try moving your breakfast out of the kitchen. We have a splendid old mahogany table, and breakfast served on its mellow gleaming surface takes on an incomparable richness. Breakfast on a cast-iron or glass-topped table in the patio or garden gives the meal a fresh, relaxed air. An unfinished pine or redwood table is a perfect background to a country-style breakfast.

· NAPKINS ·

Choose your napkins to complement the style of breakfast you're serving and the dishes and other tableware you've set out. We have a wide assortment of cloth napkins: country French blue and red checks, bright modern patterns, crisp linens, subtle pastel stripes. All of them are called into service at breakfast, sometimes matched, sometimes mixed, depending on the meal, who (if anyone) is joining us, and how bleary-eyed we were when we set the table.

There's also a supply of good quality paper napkins on hand for when we're serving breakfast to a crowd. I'll even admit to carefully folding sturdy paper towels into triangular napkins.

· TABLE COVERINGS ·

Wherever you're serving breakfast or brunch, a table covering can change its mood or style in an instant. Plastic-coated waterproof table covers are great for family or children's breakfasts. Their bright colors add a real sense for fun, and they wipe clean in an instant. For a more genteel gathering, cover your table with a fine lace cloth—placed on top of a plain-colored cloth to conceal a less-than-attractive table, or placed directly on top of a beautiful wood surface. Crisp white or pastel linens freshen the table for a spring or summer breakfast; earth-toned, rustic coverings lend warmth to a fall or winter breakfast.

Don't stop with conventional table cloths. Anything from a country quilt to a painter's dropcloth, a large unfolded road map to a sheet of butcher's paper, a tartan wool blanket to a festive rag rug, can help create a special breakfast mood.

· PLACEMATS ·

This is a matter of taste and choice: Sometimes we use them, sometimes we don't. Most of the time, they're exclusively a decorative element: neat woven straw mats for a country-style breakfast or brunch, bright yellow mats to open up sleepy eyes, subtle linen mats to soothe them. Placemats can also lend an air of formality without the need of a tablecloth. They can make cleanup easier by catching local spills, so be sure to have placemats on hand that can be wiped clean or that are machine washable.

Lynn Karlin

CENTERPIECES & DECORATIONS

No matter how simple it is, a centerpiece or other decorative item makes the final style statement on your breakfast table. It catches the eye and adds a sense of fun or romance or comfort—whatever you need to underscore the theme of a meal or the mood of the morning. Flowers are the obvious choice, but there's a world of other decorations to choose from.

· FLOWERS ·

I love to decorate a breakfast table with bright, cheery seasonal flowers. The best choices are the simplest—a handfull of daffodils, a bunch of tulips, a single carnation or rose. Save the large arrangements of flowers for the sideboard or the living room.

Keep the containers for breakfast table flowers simple, avoiding large or elaborate vases. An earthenware pitcher, a large coffee mug or a milk bottle have the right casual style. For more formal breakfasts, place the flowers in simple glass, crystal, or pottery vases. Shallow bowls holding closely clipped blossoms are another simple, beautiful approach.

Everlasting dried flowers also make a dramatic decorative statement, but I find their muted tones are used to best effect in autumn or winter.

· PLANTS ·

Other growing things also make beautiful focal points for the breakfast table. Try moving one or a few small foliage or flowering houseplants to the table for the duration of the meal. A pot of trailing ivy looks perfect against a lace tablecloth. A tray of tiny cacti is striking against a wooden table or earth-toned cloth for a summer breakfast. A cluster of potted red and white poinsettias makes an exuberant display for the holiday breakfast table.

· FOODS ·

Many breakfast ingredients themselves make delightful centerpieces. Pile white and brown eggs together in a brown twig basket that has a handle. Arrange whole fresh fruits in a large bowl or on a platter and splash them with a few drops of water so they look dewy-fresh (keep the arrangement informal-looking so guests won't need encouragement to eat them).

You can also fill a platter, bowl, or basket with whole vegetables—the same kind you've cooked for the omelet filling, perhaps. The shapes and colors of nuts in their shells provide a rich, lustrous still-life. Large chunks of cheese and whole breakfast hams or cured sausages make an impressive display that just begs to be eaten.

Brian Leatart

· ARTS, CRAFTS & *OBJETS* ·

Take a good look around your home and spot those small objects that give delight to the eye; then transfer one or more of them to the breakfast table. We've graced our table with a Mexican wooden folk-art jaguar; a small modern art brass sculpture; a terra cotta replica of a Mayan figurine; an antique railway switching signal; a beautiful piece of ivory-colored coral; a collection of carved wooden fruits and vegetables; a small dish of Venetian glass "candies."

Your breakfast or brunch table can become an expression of your family's own interests and tastes. Give the children's latest school crafts projects pride of place or let the kids choose their favorite soft toys to put on view for a special morning meal. Set out an assortment of colorful candles that you bought at the local gift shop; there's no rule that says you can't light them just because it's sunny outside. Pile old straw hats on the table, or a collection of antique bottles, or decorative jars, or sea shells. Let your imagination run wild.

BREAKFAST & BRUNCH STYLE

By choosing a particular kind of dishware and appropriate cutlery, serving dishes, cups and glassware, napkins, table coverings, and decorative touches, you can create a special mood to complement the breakfast and brunch foods you serve. Follow these suggestions for creating various breakfast styles; you'll find even more accompanying the menus in the next chapter. Use them as the starting point for developing your own unique approach to morning table settings.

or band around the rim. Sturdy clear glass dishes, widely available and inexpensive, are also a good everyday choice.

Complement your everyday dishes with sturdy tumblers or straight-sided tall glasses such as those made and widely distributed by Durand. Use glass or plain white stoneware mugs, and a simple, modern pattern of stainless steel flatware.

Set everything out on your everyday table top, or a simple, unpatterned table cloth. Set out a plain ceramic or stoneware vase of flowers to complete this fresh, clean look.

· EVERYDAY ·

Everyday breakfasts look beautiful set out on all-purpose, clean-edged tableware. Plain white or speckle-finished stoneware is a good choice; if you like, choose a pattern with a simple colored stripe

· COUNTRY ·

There are so many dishes you can choose from to achieve a country-style breakfast or brunch table. Use heavy pottery with a floral pattern or country scenes painted in shades of yellow, brown, red, and blue: if you like, mix patterns. Shops everywhere carry such pieces, imported from France, Mexico, Portugal, Spain, and elsewhere. Comb country antique stores for new dishes to add to the breakfast collection.

Coarsely woven placemats and napkins in earth tones, against a wooden table or simple table cloth, provide the perfect background. Set the table with heavy silver or stainless steel in a simple pattern, perhaps with wooden or plastic handles. Instead of tumblers, use half-pint or pint (quarter-liter or half-liter) canning jars for juice or milk. Fill an earthenware pitcher with wildflowers, or arrange an assortment of baskets on the table, filling some with eggs, others with flowers, fruits, or nuts.

· ASIAN ·

An assortment of Asian-style dinnerware can bring grace and beauty to the breakfast table. Traditional china in blue-and-white Chinese patterns looks lovely on the breakfast table. Japanese tulip bowls are perfect to hold small servings of cereal or fruit. Many manufacturers of top-line tableware offer Asian-inspired patterns. Whatever pieces you use, complement them with simple, straight-lined cutlery, or pieces with a bamboo or lotus pattern, or with ivory or plastic handles. Small Chinese tea cups, or hefty Japanese stoneware mugs, can do double duty for coffee.

Woven bamboo or rattan placemats, or gleaming brass trays, make excellent backgrounds. Choose napkins with bold blue-and-white Asian prints that complement the plates. For the centerpiece, use an assortment of ginger jars filled with flowers, or perhaps a *bonsai* tree (available today in many nurseries).

· ELEGANT ·

It's permissible, on occasion, to set the morning table with those pieces you'd usually reserve for a special dinner. Use your finest china, however simple or ornate it may be, and your best silverware. Instead of the usual glasses, serve juice or milk in crystal wine goblets.

Set everything out on the dining room table, which you've polished to gleaming perfection. Break out the silver and crystal to hold jams, sugar, cream, butter, and breakfast breads. Place fine linen napkins at each setting, rolled and held with silver or ivory napkin rings.

Charles E. Dorris/Manhattan Views

· A TOUCH OF WHIMSY ·

My favorite breakfast and brunch tableware is a shade more whimsical than most people's tastes (including, I suspect, my wife's). Over the past few years, without realizing it was happening, I've amassed a collection of plates, dishes, and other table accoutrements shaped like fruits and vegetables. Some of them are expensive pieces of artist porcelain; others are cheap souvenir-style pottery. I find all of them delightful.

I like nothing more than to use as many of them as possible at breakfast: bowls in the shape of cantaloupe halves for oatmeal, cereal, or fruit; an eggplant dish filled with whipped cream cheese and accompanied by a pair of tiny butter knives with asparagus handles; a giant pineapple pitcher for juice; matching tomato sugar bowl and creamer; corn or lemon salt and pepper shakers.

To add to the whimsy, I'll round things out with a cow creamer for milk and a butter dish shaped like a goose. I'll use bold-checked napkins, and a mixture of cutlery styles. For hot drinks, I'll offer an assortment from our mug collection: hand-thrown pottery; beautifully decorated English Denby stoneware; a commemorative from Prince Andrew's marriage to Fergie; a mug from a stand that sells buffalo burgers in San Jose, California; a Superman mug; a Tyrannosaurus Rex mug from the local dinosaur museum; and several of the jolly animal mugs produced by Taylor & Ng.

The message here is, simply, let your own sense of fun rule!

· AVANT-GARDE ·

There are so many adventurous new designs in tableware available today, ready to add excitement to your breakfast table: deep black, bright turquoise, or cherry-red plates with glossy or matte finishes; porcelain painted to resemble coral, or blue or black marble; plates decorated in bold, op-art patterns; one-of-a-kind pieces and sets; striking glassware and silverware in wild geometric designs.

Don't be afraid to use any of these pieces at breakfast. Let them, in fact, inspire you to bold, elegant presentations of the foods you serve. Go crazy and do an entire table in avant-garde style, or let one or two pieces provide eye-catching contrast to a more sedate setting.

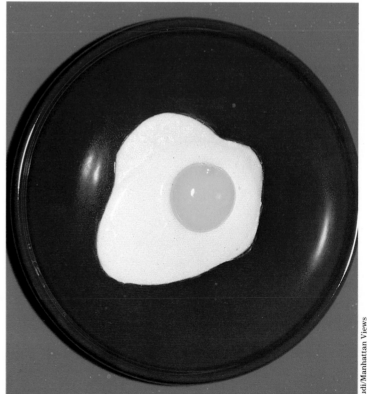

Oudi/Manhattan Views

SECTION III:
BREAKFAST & BRUNCH MENUS & RECIPES

SPECIAL MOMENTS

FAMILY BREAKFAST FOR FOUR

FRESH-SQUEEZED ORANGE JUICE

SCRAMBLED EGGS WITH FIVE CHEESES

BACON

RAISIN PUMPERNICKEL TOAST WITH CREAM CHEESE

OR BUTTER

FRESH CHUNKY STRAWBERRY SPREAD (PAGE 29)

MILK AND COFFEE

Weekends may be the only time most families have to enjoy breakfast together. The style should be decidedly casual. Pajamas, nightgowns, and bathrobes are the preferred attire. Set the kitchen or dining room table with everyday plates and silverware, the plainer the better. Pick some flowers from the garden and put them in a simple glass or earthenware vase. Bring in the morning paper and the kids' favorite magazines and stack them there on the table for browsing, with one important rule: that people share what they're reading, and use it as a starting point for family conversation. Or tune in a favorite radio station.

The food reflects this homey, casual style. Orange juice (fresh-squeezed or from the supermarket) and milk should sit on the table in large pitchers; make a pot of coffee in advance for grownups and older children, and have it on the table in a thermos pitcher. Scrambled Eggs with Five Cheeses is a rich, indulgent threat that's easily prepared; young children—under close parental supervision—might enjoy standing on a sturdy chair or stool and stirring the eggs as they thicken. Buy a good loaf of raisin pumpernickel bread the night before on the way home, and have it ready to toast and spread with softened cream cheese or butter.

Judd Pilossof

SCRAMBLED EGGS WITH FIVE CHEESES

Use any combination of cheeses you like, but try, as I've done with the ingredients here, to create a good balance of tastes and textures in the cheeses you choose.

2 tablespoons unsalted butter

8 eggs, beaten until slightly foamy

2 tablespoons garlic-herb cream cheese

¼ cup shredded sharp Cheddar cheese

¼ cup shredded smoked mozzarella

¼ cup shredded Monterey jack cheese

¼ cup grated Parmesan cheese

½ teaspoon freshly ground black pepper

2 tablespoons chopped fresh parsley

Melt the butter in a large skillet or saucepan over moderate to low heat. Add the eggs and cook them gently, stirring and scraping frequently.

As the eggs just begin to thicken, add the cream cheese and stir until it melts and blends into the eggs. When the eggs are fairly thick but still very loose and creamy, add the remaining cheeses. Stir as the cheeses melt. Continue stirring and scraping the egg-and-cheese mixture until thick and creamy. Season with pepper and serve on heated plates, garnished with parsley.

Makes 4 servings.

BREAKFAST FOR ONE

WHOLE BABY MANGO WITH LIME

SOUFFLE CUP BUTTERMILK BLUEBERRY MUFFIN

WITH MARMALADE

COFFEE

More and more people today, so demographic surveys tell us, live on their own. And when there's only yourself to feed, the easiest meal of the day to overlook is breakfast.

This simple menu makes breakfast for one a pleasure. Since many single breakfasters are young working adults, it's quickly prepared and eaten, yet gives a healthy start to a busy day. The featured recipe is a large muffin baked in an individual soufflé dish. You can mix the batter, put it in the oven, peel and slice a whole baby mango (or other choice fruit) and start the coffee in a few minutes before you hit the shower; be quick about washing and dressing, and breakfast will be ready by the time you slip on your shoes.

Start the day with a touch of class. Serve the muffin on a good china bread plate, with crystal dishes of marmalade and butter. Place a single rosebud in a crystal vase at the top of your individual setting. Put a favorite record on the stereo, and pamper yourself with fifteen minutes of pleasure before you start the working day.

SOUFFLÉ CUP BUTTERMILK BLUEBERRY MUFFIN

1 tablespoon fresh or defrosted frozen blueberries

½ cup all-purpose flour

2 teaspoons sugar

1 teaspoon baking powder

Pinch of salt

½ small egg, lightly beaten

2 teaspoons melted unsalted butter

¼ cup buttermilk

Preheat the oven to 400°F.

Rinse the blueberries and toss them with a teaspoon or so of the flour to coat them lightly. Set aside.

In a mixing bowl, stir together the flour, sugar, baking powder, and salt. Make a well in the center, add the egg and the butter and then briefly stir them into the dry ingredients with just enough of the buttermilk to make a thick, lumpy batter. Fold in the blueberries.

Pour the batter into a greased 1-cup soufflé dish. Bake for about 20 minutes, or until the muffin is well risen, golden brown, and a wooden toothpick inserted into its center comes out clean. Unmold the muffin and serve it hot with butter and marmalade.

Makes 1 large muffin.

ROMANTIC BREAKFAST FOR TWO

BLOOD ORANGE JUICE MIMOSAS

OMELETS WITH SALMON CAVIAR

TOASTED EGG BREAD WITH BUTTER

COFFEE OR TEA

Any day can be Valentine's Day with this wonderfully indulgent breakfast for two. It's designed to be served on a tray—in bed.

Surprise your mate by slipping off to the kitchen while he or she still slumbers. Start the coffee going. Then prepare the omelets, and make the toast with thinly sliced good commercial egg bread. If blood oranges are available, by all means use them for your breakfast juice; their passionate red hue is perfect for this meal. Pour the juice into champagne flutes and, if it's a morning for lingering, add an equal amount of champagne to each glass to make mimosas.

Set a large, pretty tray with a small vase of wildflowers, good silverware, floral-print or pastel-pink napkins, and your prettiest country-style china dishes, cups, and saucers. Put Vivaldi or Mozart on the stereo and let your mate wake up to beautiful music and a romantic meal.

OMELETS WITH SALMON CAVIAR

Most supermarket gourmet sections now carry small, 2-ounce jars of salmon caviar or roe. The sparkling, orange-pink eggs have a mild, slightly salty flavor reminiscent of smoked salmon. They're surprisingly inexpensive for the touch of elegance they bring.

6 eggs

¼ teaspoon salt

2 tablespoons unsalted butter

5 tablespoons sour cream

5 tablespoons salmon caviar

1 tablespoon chopped fresh chives

Break 3 of the eggs into a mixing bowl and beat them lightly. Stir in half of the salt.

Heat an omelet pan over moderately high heat. Then add the 1 tablespoon of butter and immediately swirl the pan as it melts; pour in the eggs.

As the eggs begin to set, use a fork to gently and carefully lift and push the eggs from the edges toward the center, letting the still-liquid egg run underneath. Continue until the omelet is almost completely set but still somewhat moist in the center.

Spread 2 tablespoons of the sour cream over half of the omelet, and top it with 2 tablespoons of the caviar. Firmly grasp the handle of the pan and give the pan a small but firm shake to loosen the omelet. Then slide it out onto a heated serving plate, flipping the pan as you do so to fold the omelet in half over the filling. Keep the omelet warm.

Repeat with the remaining eggs, salt, butter, and 2 tablespoons each of the sour cream and caviar. Top each omelet with some of the remaining sour cream and caviar, and a scattering of chives.

Makes 2 servings.

POWER BREAKFAST FOR SIX

GRAPEFRUIT JUICE

SCRAMBLED EGGS WITH CHOPPED FRESH CHIVES

BROILED TENDERLOIN BREAKFAST STEAKS

CORNMEAL CHILI MUFFINS

JAMAICAN BLUE MOUNTAIN COFFEE

A power breakfast is where talk is tough and deals are driven speedily to conclusion. The setting should suggest a no-nonsense approach to getting things done, and the food should speak of strength and ambition.

If you're in a line of work that allows you to call a power breakfast at your home, do so! Think of what a power play it is to summon people from their homes to yours at a pre-work hour, forcing them to get out of bed at least half an hour earlier than usual. (If you can't pull off such a power move, cut all the ingredients in the menu by two-thirds and share a power breakfast with your mate, to fortify you both for a hard-working day.)

If you have dishware in shades of gray or black, use it; it speaks of serious business. Have good, plain, heavy coffee mugs ready for rare Jamaican Blue Mountain Coffee, and stainless steel cutlery in clean, sleek lines. If you want a touch of color, use strong, macho flowers—anthuriums are perfect. (And, speaking of macho, a woman can throw a power breakfast just as skillfully as any man.) Have at least two copies of the *Wall Street*

Sam Sweezy/Robert Flack and Associates, designers

Journal on the table. If notes need to be taken, place a yellow legal pad and a #2 pencil at each setting.

Steak is a powerful choice for the main course. Choose an expensive but not overly fancy cut that is easily divided into breakfast-sized portions; beef tenderloin is ideal. Prepare the scrambled eggs before your colleagues are due to arrive: Keep them warm in their pan by covering it and placing it inside a large pan half-filled with hot but not boiling water; have some chopped fresh chives ready as a garnish. Cornmeal Chili Muffins have an earthy quality that helps set the right tone. You can easily mix the batter and set the muffins to baking about five minutes before the meeting is due to start, so they'll be ready around the time the steaks are done; keep them warm in a silver or stainless steel bowl, lined with a large plain-colored napkin. Have the broiler preheated and ready for the steaks. *Don't* give people a choice; you'll grill them all medium-rare and they'll like them that way—or else.

BROILED TENDERLOIN BREAKFAST STEAKS

1½ tablespoons unsalted butter, softened

1 tablespoon Worcestershire sauce

Salt and freshly ground black pepper

3 pounds beef tenderloin, cut into 6 steaks

Preheat the broiler.

With a fork, mash the butter together with the Worcestershire sauce and salt and pepper to taste. Spread the butter evenly on both sides of each steak.

When the broiler is hot, place the steaks on the broiler tray. Cook them about 2 inches from the heat for 3 to 4 minutes per side for medium-rare.

Makes 6 servings.

CORNMEAL CHILI MUFFINS

If you want to up the status of this recipe, try making it with blue cornmeal, now available in many gourmet stores.

1 cup all-purpose flour

1 cup yellow (or blue) cornmeal

1 tablespoon baking powder

1 tablespoon sugar

1 cup milk

2 eggs, lightly beaten

¼ cup (½ stick) butter, melted

¼ cup honey, at room temperature

3 tablespoons chopped canned green chilies, thoroughly drained

Preheat the oven to 400°F.

In a mixing bowl, stir together the flour, cornmeal, baking powder, and sugar. In a separate bowl, stir together the milk, eggs, and butter. Add the liquid ingredients and the honey to the dry ingredients and stir just until the batter is lumpy. Stir in the chopped chilies. Do not overmix.

Spoon the batter into 12 greased muffin cups, filling them two thirds full. Bake for about 20 minutes, or until the muffins are well risen, golden, and a wooden toothpick inserted into the center of one comes out clean.

Makes 12 muffins.

PICNIC BRUNCH FOR FOUR

SELECTION OF FRESH FRUITS

SPICED APPLESAUCE BREAD

WITH WHIPPED CREAM CHEESE AND

CHOPPED DATES

CINNAMON COFFEE

When the weather's warm and the skies are clear, it's the perfect time to take brunch outdoors. Pack simple foods that you don't have to worry about, with fresh, clean tastes that reflect the weather.

Bake the Spiced Applesauce Bread an hour or so before you set out. After it has cooled a bit, pack it in foil or an airtight container to keep it moist and fresh. In separate containers, put whipped cream cheese and chopped dates to use as toppings for the bread when you slice it (be sure to pack a bread knife!). Choose the best, juiciest fruits of the season: grapes, peaches, plums, nectarines—anything that's easy to eat by hand. Brew a pot of cinnamon coffee and seal it in a thermos pitcher; put cream or half-and-half and sugar in small containers with tight-fitting lids. Have sturdy plastic plates and old knockabout cutlery, simple gingham napkins and a matching tablecloth or an old blanket to spread on the ground. Stow the entire picnic contents in a wicker hamper or basket, tuck in the morning paper or a favorite book of poetry, and you're ready to enjoy the pleasures of a fine morning.

SPICED APPLESAUCE BREAD

1 cup all-purpose flour

½ cup whole-wheat flour

½ teaspoon salt

1 teaspoon baking soda

1 cup applesauce

6 tablespoons (¾ stick) unsalted butter, melted

2 eggs, lightly beaten

½ teaspoon cinnamon

½ teaspoon powdered ginger

¼ teaspoon allspice

¼ teaspoon nutmeg

½ cup golden raisins

Preheat the oven to 350°F.

In a mixing bowl, stir together the flours, salt, and baking soda. In a separate bowl, stir together the applesauce, butter, eggs, and spices. Stir the applesauce mixture into the dry ingredients just until a smooth batter forms. Mix in the raisins.

Pour the batter into a greased 9-by-5-by-3-inch loaf pan. Bake the bread for about 1 hour, until a thin skewer or wooden toothpick inserted into its center comes out clean.

Invert the baking pan onto a wire rack to unmold the bread. Let it cool slightly before wrapping it. Cut into slices about ½ inch thick.

Makes 1 loaf.

CHILDREN'S BREAKFAST PARTY FOR EIGHT

FRESH FRUIT ARRANGED IN SMILING FACES

CHOCOLATE CHIP ANIMAL PANCAKES

WITH ASSORTED SYRUPS

MILK AND HOT CHOCOLATE

Kids are at their best in the morning—well-rested, cheerful, and far easier to handle than they are from midday on. Yet, inexplicably, most children's parties are thrown in the afternoon, when the kids are likely to be at their crabbiest.

Try making the next children's party you throw a *breakfast*. The first meal of the day offers so many more opportunities for whimsy, as the pancakes in this menu demonstrate. Use good-sized cookie cutters, available in most kitchenware stores, and make sure they're metal cookie cutters: plastic ones will melt in the skillet! Get the kids to eat some fresh fruit by arranging berries and bananas in smiling face designs (bananas sliced lengthwise for the smiles, strawberry nose, blueberry eyes—use your imagination).

Set the party time for mid-morning—say ten or ten-thirty. Put brightly colored, easy-to-clean plastic placemats and dishware on the table, or use sturdy plastic-coated paper party plates if you wish. Have cups with spill-proof lids on hand for the younger tots. Make a centerpiece display of the child-of-honor's favorite dolls, cars, or action figures.

CHOCOLATE CHIP ANIMAL PANCAKES

1½ cups all-purpose flour

¼ cup unsweetened cocoa powder

3 tablespoons sugar

1 tablespoon baking powder

½ teaspoon salt

1 egg, lightly beaten

1¼ cups milk

3 tablespoons unsalted butter, melted

½ cup semisweet chocolate chips

Confectioner's sugar (optional)

In a mixing bowl, stir together the flour, cocoa, sugar, baking powder, and salt. In a separate bowl, stir together the egg, milk, and butter. Stir the liquids into the dry ingredients, mixing just long enough to make a smooth batter. Transfer the batter to a large measuring cup or pitcher with a pouring lip.

Lightly grease a large skillet or griddle over moderate heat. Lightly grease the inside cutting edges of large metal animal-shaped cookie cutters; place the cutters in the skillet and pour in just enough of the batter to fill in their outlines. When bubbles begin to appear on the surfaces of the pancakes, sprinkle a teaspoon or so of chocolate chips over each pancake. Continue cooking until their surfaces are covered with bubbles, then lift away the cutters and use a spatula to carefully flip the pancakes and cook them on the other side. Transfer to a heated platter and keep warm.

Repeat the procedure with the remaining batter and chocolate chips. If you (or the kids) like, sift a little confectioner's sugar over the pancakes before serving.

Makes 8 servings.

Peter Poulides/Manhattan Views

H E A L T H   F O O D
B R E A K F A S T
F O R   T W O

FRESH PAPAYA

FIVE-GRAIN BRAN MUFFINS

HOMEMADE YOGURT (PAGE 71)

WITH WHEAT GERM AND HONEY

DECAFFEINATED COFFEE OR MINT TEA

So many people skip breakfast when they're trying to cut down on their eating. If you're really trying to be health conscious, the right approach is to eat a breakfast composed of really healthy foods. That's what you'll find in this menu. There's a high-fiber, five-grain muffin; fresh papaya, which includes the digestion-aiding enzyme papayan; yogurt, whose benefits are well known; all topped with honey and wheat germ (rich in Vitamin E). And you have your choice of decaffeinated coffee (make sure it's Swiss water-processed, without the use of chemicals), or one of the many commercial mint tea blends now available, whose sprightly flavors can really brighten a morning.

Wear your jogging suit to the table if you like, but don't be an ascetic about your breakfast setting. Include a vase of bright flowers and your most beautiful tableware to reinforce the idea that healthy morning eating can be stylish and fun.

FIVE-GRAIN BRAN MUFFINS

Here's the grain countdown: wheat (all-purpose flour for lightness, whole wheat, and bran); corn; rice; millet; and sunflower seeds.

¾ cup all-purpose flour

¼ cup whole wheat flour

1 tablespoon rice flour

½ cup natural bran

1 tablespoon cornmeal

1 tablespoon millet

1 tablespoon shelled, unroasted sunflower seeds

1 teaspoon baking powder

¼ teaspoon salt

1 cup Homemade Yogurt (page 71)

¼ cup seedless raisins

¼ cup vegetable oil

¼ cup honey

Preheat the oven to 425°F.

In a mixing bowl, stir together the flours, bran, cornmeal, millet, sunflower seeds, baking powder and salt. Stir in the yogurt, raisins, oil and honey just until the dry ingredients are moistened.

Spoon the batter into 6 greased muffin cups. Bake until well risen and browned, and a wooden toothpick inserted into the center of a muffin comes out clean, about 25 minutes.

Makes 6 muffins.

DO-IT-YOURSELF OMELET PARTY FOR TWELVE

ASSORTED FRESH FRUIT JUICES

PLATTER OF FRESH SEASONAL FRUITS

OMELETS WITH ASSORTED FILLINGS

CHUNKY SPANISH FILLING

CHICKEN LIVER SAUTÉ

FRESH-BAKED MUFFINS

WITH BUTTER AND JAMS

COFFEE AND TEA

I can't think of a more pleasant way to entertain than to have your guests over and let *them* do all the cooking. Well, *most* of the cooking. In this menu, suitable for a Sunday brunch at any time of year, all you do is set out a beautiful container piled high with three eggs per guest—a wicker basket or napkin-lined country-style pottery bowl would be ideal—and an assortment of fillings. Have at least two well-seasoned omelet pans at the ready, with good pot holders, along with several medium-sized bowls and forks or whisks for beating the eggs; keep a small pitcher of melted butter nearby for greasing the pans. Set out bowls with an assortment of fillings—two or three kinds of shredded cheese, julienned ham, crumbled bacon, chopped fresh herbs, cooked bay shrimp or crabmeat, steamed asparagus tips, roasted pepper strips, or whatever seasonal delights strike your fancy. I've included two cooked filling recipes here

if you want to add even more variety to the selection.

If your kitchen and stove are large enough, you can let the guests do the cooking right there. If space is at a premium, set up portable gas or electric burners in the dining room or, if the weather is nice, outdoors. Stack plates next to the cooking units, so the guests can slip their omelets right from the pan to plate.

Country style is the perfect theme. You might like to set filling bowls inside an assortment of small baskets. Cover the table with an old, pretty bedspread or quilt, and use heavy pottery dishware and mugs—mix and match patterns if you like. Put a selection of fruit juices out in large, heavy pitchers, and sliced seasonal fruit on a large platter. Fill a big, napkin-lined basket with your favorite home-baked (or store-bought) muffins. Dried flowers are an ideal final decorative touch.

All that's left for you to do is cook your own omelet. You get to eat first; after all, you have to demonstrate the omelet making technique (see page 56) before your guests go to work.

Lynn Karlin

CHUNKY SPANISH FILLING

3 tablespoons olive oil

3 medium garlic cloves, finely chopped

2 medium onions, coarsely chopped

2 green bell peppers, stemmed, seeded, and cut into ½-inch chunks

1 (28 ounce) can whole tomatoes, drained

1 tablespoon double-concentrate tomato paste or 2 tablespoons regular tomato paste

½ tablespoon sugar

1 teaspoon dried oregano

1 teaspoon dried basil

1 bay leaf

¾ teaspoon salt

½ teaspoon black pepper

In a large skillet or saucepan, heat the oil over medium heat. Add the garlic and onion and sauté until tender, about 3 minutes.

Add all the remaining ingredients and simmer briskly, stirring occasionally and breaking up the tomatoes with a wooden spoon, until the sauce is thick, about 15 minutes. Keep warm in a covered ovenproof dish.

Makes 12 servings.

CHICKEN LIVER SAUTÉ

1 tablespoon vegetable oil

4 strips bacon, cut crosswise into ¼-inch pieces

1 medium onion, finely chopped

12 chicken livers, trimmed and cut into ½-inch chunks

¼ cup dry white wine

Salt and freshly ground black pepper

1 tablespoon chopped fresh parsley

In a large skillet, heat the vegetable oil over medium to low heat and sauté the bacon until golden brown but still somewhat soft, about 3 minutes. Drain off all but about 1 tablespoon of the fat and add the onion. Sauté for 30 seconds.

Add the chicken livers and sauté just until they lose their pink color and are firm, 2 to 3 minutes. Add the wine, raise the heat slightly, and stir and scrape to deglaze the pan deposits. When all but about a tablespoon of the wine has evaporated, season to taste and sprinkle on the parsley. Keep warm in a covered ovenproof dish.

Makes 12 servings.

INTERNATIONAL BREAKFASTS & BRUNCHES

BRITISH BREAKFAST FOR EIGHT

ORANGE OR TOMATO JUICE

MIXED GRILL WITH FRIED BREAD

CREAMED KIPPERS

SCRAMBLED EGGS

TOASTED ENGLISH MUFFINS

MARMALADE

ENGLISH BREAKFAST TEA WITH MILK OR LEMON

COFFEE

"To eat well in England," wrote the novelist Somerset Maugham, "you should have breakfast three times a day." A full English breakfast *is* one of the heartiest meals you can eat. It speaks of weekends in stately homes, of guests toddling downstairs to a civilized late-morning repast designed to satisfy appetites sharpened by robust walks in the brisk country air.

This menu offers the full bounty of the British table. It is best served on a weekend, when there's more time to digest it at a leisurely pace. If you like, go all out for the presentation. Set out your finest bone china, including teacups and saucers,

with polished silverware and heavy linen napkins. Put marmalade in small crystal, china, or silver jam pots. Daffodils, those quintessential English flowers, will look perfectly at home center-table in your most elegant vase.

If you want to serve a crowd, you can double (or even triple) the quantities here. In that case, keep the food warm in chafing dishes on a sideboard; stack plates, silver and napkins alongside, so guests can help themselves when they wander in.

And speaking of guests, tell yours to dress in good English country style—cords or flannels for the men, Laura Ashley-style prints for the women. Have copies of the *Times*, the *Guardian*, the *Telegraph*, or perhaps *Country Life* set out on a side table for them to browse through if they wish. Add to the English country atmosphere with some music by Elgar, Walton, or Britten, or perhaps a recording of English madrigals.

Brian Leatart

MIXED GRILL WITH FRIED BREAD

The mixed grill—usually consisting of a sausage, a strip of bacon and a sautéed kidney—is a breakfast staple in Britain. A lot of butcher shops that specialize in freshly made sausages offer authentic English ''bangers''—plump pork-and-bread sausages. If they're not available, select the plumpest fresh sausages you can find, or use a large, good-quality commercial sausage. The bacon should be thick-cut back slices. If your guests aren't keen on kidneys (admittedly, an acquired taste), substitute more sausages and bacon.

You'll need at least two large skillets to fry up these ingredients all at once.

8 large fresh pork sausages, punctured with a fork in 2 or 3 places

8 thick strips back bacon

4 veal kidneys, trimmed and cut in halves horizontally

4 tablespoons (½ stick) unsalted butter

4 (½-inch-thick) slices white bread, crusts trimmed and discarded, cut into 4 triangles each

Preheat the oven to 300°F.

Pour about ½ inch of water into two large skillets and place the sausages in them over moderate heat. As the water begins to evaporate, turn the sausages. Continue cooking them as their fat renders and they begin to fry and brown.

When the sausages are moderately browned, add the bacon to the skillets. Fry it until golden brown and crisp. Remove the bacon and sausages to a covered ovenproof dish, and keep them warm in the oven.

Add the kidneys to the skillets and fry them in the rendered sausage and bacon fat until lightly browned, about 2 minutes per side. Remove them to the covered dish in the oven and pour off most of the bacon fat.

Melt the butter with the thin film of fat that remains in the skillets. Add the bread triangles and fry them until deep golden brown, 2 to 3 minutes per side.

Drain the meats and bread on paper towels and serve immediately.

Makes 8 servings.

Britain on View

CREAMED KIPPERS

The kippered herring, or ''kipper,'' is a plump, delicately flavored breakfast fish, the result of brine soaking and a brief smoking. If you can't get kippers, substitute smoked trout in this recipe.

Serve the creamed kippers over buttered English muffins.

4 tablespoons (½ stick) unsalted butter

½ pound mushrooms, cut into ¼-inch slices

1 medium onion, finely chopped

1 small bell pepper, cut into ¼-inch dice

4 tablespoons all-purpose flour

½ cup medium-dry sherry

3 cups milk

8 kippers, completely boned, flesh flaked

1 tablespoon lemon juice

1 teaspoon cayenne pepper

Salt and freshly ground black pepper

Melt the butter in a large saucepan over moderate heat. Add the mushrooms, onion, and bell pepper, and sauté, stirring occasionally, until all the liquid from the mushrooms has evaporated and the vegetables are lightly browned, about 10 minutes.

Sprinkle the vegetables with the flour and sauté about 2 minutes more. Add the sherry, raise the heat, and stir and scrape with a wooden spoon to dissolve the pan deposits. Continue simmering briskly until the sherry has been reduced by about two-thirds.

Add the milk and bring it to a boil. Reduce the heat to a bare simmer, gently stir in the kippers, and continue simmering until the mixture is thick and creamy, 15 to 20 minutes more. Stir in the lemon juice, cayenne, and salt and pepper to taste and serve immediately.

Makes 8 servings.

FRENCH BREAKFAST FOR FOUR

FROMAGE FRAIS WITH SEASONAL BERRIES

CROISSANTS OR CRUSTY ROLLS

CAFE AU LAIT

One of the delights of breakfast on the Continent is the creamy, slightly tangy fresh cheese you are often served. You can spread it, like a cream cheese, on your crusty breakfast rolls, or eat it straight—plain or with jam or fresh berries.

While the recipe in this menu does not make the fresh cheese from scratch—a more complicated task that even most French cooks will not face—it does allow you to produce near-authentic results with a minimum of effort. You *will* need a large porcelain cheese mold, or several small ones, with small holes in the bottom so the cheese can drain (a fine sieve will do in a pinch); and you'll need some cheesecloth. The French frequently use heart-shaped molds, and call the resulting dish *coeur à la creme*.

Needless to say, the table should be appropriately set with French porcelain, if you have it, or any delicate, pretty dishware. Have extra-large coffee cups on hand to hold the *cafe au lait*—equal parts of strong black coffee and hot milk; or replace your usual coffee cups or mugs with deep cereal bowls, to be held with both hands while sipping.

Use a lace tablecloth to add to the refined French air, and fill a few small, low vases or tiny pitchers or bowls with the most delicate seasonal flowers you can find. Listen to Edith Piaf, if you have one of her records (they're worth buying), or some Debussy or Ravel.

Jerry Howard/Positive Images

F R O M A G E   F R A I S
W I T H   S E A S O N A L
B E R R I E S

1 cup large curd cottage cheese

1¾ cups whipping cream

2 teaspoons confectioner's sugar

2 egg whites

2 cups strawberries, raspberries, or blueberries

In a food processor, process the cottage cheese with 1¼ cups of the cream and the sugar until smooth and light.

In a separate bowl, beat the egg whites until soft peaks form. Add them to the processor and pulse them into the cheese.

Line a cheese mold or fine-mesh sieve with a double thickness of cheesecloth. Spoon in the cheese mixture and set the mold or sieve over a large bowl. Refrigerate overnight. The next morning, discard the drained liquid, unmold the sieve and serve, surrounded by fresh berries.

Makes 4 servings.

MEXICAN
BRUNCH
FOR FOUR

PLATTER OF TROPICAL FRUITS WITH LIME

HUEVOS RANCHEROS

MEXICAN HOT CHOCOLATE

A Mexican brunch of huevos rancheros—ranch-style eggs—is a complete morning meal on a single plate. You have your bread—in this case, a crisp tortilla. There are beans and, in the recipe that follows, crisp bacon. Then the eggs, cheese, avocado, salsa, sour cream. . . . It's no wonder that huevos rancheros makes an excellent, popular brunch dish; clean your plate, and you're full until dinner time.

Begin this menu with a selection of tropical fruits—mango, papaya and pineapple, served sliced with wedges of lime. To drink, offer coffee with cinnamon or, the traditional favorite, cups of thick, fragrant Mexican hot chocolate.

Set the table with rustic Mexican pottery in primary colors, and have heavy mugs on hand to hold the chocolate. Spread a coarsely woven, brightly colored tablecloth, with matching napkins; or, if you bought one on a past visit to Mexico, cover the table with a gaily striped *serape*. Put large, vivid flowers—anemones are perfect—in a hefty earthenware jug. I also like to decorate the table with a few pieces of Mexican folk art—terra cotta replicas of Mayan effigies, or vividly painted wooden animals.

Jeff McNamara/James Goslee III, stylist

HUEVOS
RANCHEROS

You have a lot of options with huevos rancheros, so feel free to adapt this recipe and create your own. This version uses canned refried beans, which are widely available and every bit as good as those you'd spend hours making from scratch; if you want to avoid the lard that's present in most refried beans, seek out one of the commercially available varieties that use vegetable oil instead, labelled "vegetarian-style." Or substitute canned kidney beans, pinto beans, or black beans. Instead of the crumbled bacon in this recipe, you might want to fry up some Mexican chorizo sausage and crumble it over the tostada; or go meatless, if that's your inclination.

This recipe also uses corn tortillas; if you like, substitute flour tortillas. Here, the tortillas are baked until crisp, for a lighter effect; you can also deep-fry them in 375°F oil for 30 seconds to 1 minute.

You also have the choice of mashing up the avocado with some salsa, lemon and sour cream to make a guacamole topping, though I prefer the look of elegant, thin slices of avocado. And you can use one of the fresh salsas available at most supermarkets, or a good chunky salsa from a jar.

4 large corn tortillas

8 strips bacon

2 (16-ounce) cans refried beans

8 eggs

1 large avocado, cut lengthwise into thin slices

½ cup sour cream

¾ cup tomato salsa

12 large pitted black olives, sliced

3 tablespoons coarsely chopped cilantro leaves

Preheat the oven to 400°F.

Put the tortillas in the oven and toast them until golden brown and crisp, about 2 minutes, watching them carefully to prevent burning.

In a large skillet, fry the bacon until crisp. Drain the bacon strips on paper towels; pour about a tablespoon of the fat into a medium saucepan, leaving the remaining fat in the skillet. Cook the

beans in the saucepan over medium heat, until heated through; meanwhile, fry the eggs sunny-side-up in the skillet.

Place a tortilla on each serving plate. Spoon the beans on top of each tortilla, spreading them evenly. Crumble 2 strips of bacon over each serving and top with 2 fried eggs. Garnish each serving with slices of avocado, a large dollop of sour cream, a generous serving of salsa, sliced olives, and, if you like, a scattering of cilantro leaves.

Makes 4 servings.

M E X I C A N   H O T   C H O C O L A T E

8 ounces bittersweet chocolate, broken into pieces

3 tablespoons honey

½ tablespoon cinnamon

¼ teaspoon nutmeg

4 cups milk

Put the chocolate, honey, cinnamon, and nutmeg in a medium saucepan over the lowest heat possible. As the chocolate melts, stir it continuously to blend it with the other ingredients.

Slowly stir in the milk. Raise the heat and bring the mixture to a boil, stirring continuously. Then immediately reduce the heat and, with a wire whisk or an egg beater, carefully but vigorously beat the mixture until it is frothy. Pour into heated mugs.

Makes 4 servings.

JEWISH DELI BREAKFAST FOR SIX

FRESHLY SQUEEZED GRAPEFRUIT JUICE

SCRAMBLED EGGS WITH LOX AND ONIONS

TOASTED BAGEL ASSORTMENT

WITH CREAM CHEESE OR BUTTER

COFFEE WITH PLENTY OF HOT MILK

Nu? You're not having any breakfast? Sit. Have a toasted bagel. Some cream cheese, maybe. Look, just let me make you a little scrambled eggs, I'll throw in a little lox, some chopped onion—make it taste good. What do you mean, no juice? Take a little fresh grapefruit. I squeezed it myself. It's good for you, cuts the fat.

For the Jewish mother in all of us, breakfast means comforting food, and lots of it. This menu combines some Jewish deli favorites, and its flavors are hearty and satisfying. It's also easy to prepare. Buy an assortment of bagels—water, egg, onion, sesame, pumpernickel, etc.—at the supermarket, a deli, or a bagel shop (most good-sized cities have them) the night before. All you have to do in the morning is squeeze the juice, brew the coffee, scramble the eggs, and split and toast the bagels.

My grandparents often served such dairy breakfasts on glass dishes, and I still think these foods look terrifically clean and beautiful served on glass atop a crisp white tablecloth. Set out glass tumblers for the juice, glass mugs for the coffee, and a little glass pitcher to hold hot milk. To enhance the experience, serve this breakfast on a Sunday morning, after you've gone out to pick up the Sunday *New York Times* (no matter what part of the country you live in, most newsstands will carry it on Sundays). Spread the paper out on the table and you'll *really* feel like you're breakfasting in a New York City deli.

Lynn Karlin

SCRAMBLED EGGS WITH LOX & ONIONS

6 tablespoons (¾ stick) unsalted butter

2 medium onions, coarsely chopped

½ pound sliced lox (smoked salmon), cut into ½-inch pieces

18 eggs, lightly beaten

½ teaspoon salt

Freshly ground white pepper

In a very large skillet (or 2 smaller skillets), melt 4 tablespoons of the butter over moderate heat. Add the onions and sauté them, stirring frequently, until they begin to turn golden brown, 5 to 7 minutes. Add the lox pieces and sauté about 1 minute more, just until the lox turns opaque. Remove the lox and onions from the skillet and set them aside.

Reduce the heat to low and melt the remaining butter in the skillet. Add the eggs and salt. Cook the eggs, stirring and scraping frequently, until they are thick but still fairly moist, at least 10 minutes. Stir in the lox and onions and continue cooking, stirring, and scraping, until the eggs are thick and creamy. Serve on heated plates and season to taste with white pepper.

Makes 6 servings.

ITALIAN-STYLE BREAKFAST FOR FOUR

SEGMENTED ORANGES DRIZZLED WITH HONEY

ITALIAN BREAKFAST PASTA

CRUSTY ROLLS WITH BUTTER

CAFFE LATTE

To be honest, I've never had pasta served for breakfast in Italy, though I'm sure some enterprising Italian has put leftover spaghetti to such an excellent, economical use. But I *have* eaten pasta at one of the best breakfast spots in Los Angeles, Hugo's, a combination delicatessen and veal butcher shop that starts serving meals at 6:30 a.m. The recipe here is my own interpretation of their many variations on breakfast pasta.

Serve it with true Italian breakfast accompaniments (which, for most Italians, make up the

Fred Lyon/Wheeler Pictures

morning meal in its entirety): good, crusty rolls, preferably sourdough; and *caffe latte*—freshly brewed, dark-roasted coffee (ask your local coffee merchant for Italian or Espresso roast), brewed extra-strong (use an espresso machine, or just add an extra spoonful to your drip filter) and served with equal parts of hot milk.

Cover the breakfast table with a large-checkered cloth and set out matching napkins. For an attractive visual pun on the main course, you might want to use extra-large dried tube pasta such as canneloni or manicotti as napkin rings, and continue the theme by decorating the table with glass jars filled with different pasta shapes. Use good, heavy country-style pottery plates, or a clean Italian-modern design with a simple stripe or two around the rim. Make sure you include a large spoon at each setting, to help guests twirl their pasta.

Brian Leatart

ITALIAN BREAKFAST PASTA

4 cups cooked spaghetti or linguini

4 tablespoons (½ stick) unsalted butter

2 medium garlic cloves, finely chopped

8 eggs, well beaten

½ cup Parmesan cheese

3 tablespoons chopped parsley

Freshly ground black pepper

While the pasta is cooking, melt the butter in a large skillet over low to moderate heat. Add the garlic cloves and sauté them just until they barely begin to brown, about 3 minutes.

Drain the cooked pasta thoroughly, and immediately toss it in the butter. Add the eggs and ¼ cup of the Parmesan, raise the heat slightly, and cook the pasta and eggs together, stirring continuously, until the eggs are thick and have formed curds that cling to the pasta. Stir in the chopped parsley.

Transfer the pasta to individual wide, shallow serving bowls and serve with extra Parmesan and plenty of black pepper.

Makes 4 servings.

RUSSIAN-STYLE BRUNCH FOR SIX

STEWED PRUNES IN HEAVY SYRUP

FRUIT JUICE

BUCKWHEAT BLINI

WITH SCRAMBLED EGGS

CRUMBLED BACON

CAVIAR

SOUR CREAM AND CHIVES

SMOKED FISH

SLICED CHEESES

ASSORTED JAMS

SOFT BUTTER

COFFEE

HOT TEA IN A GLASS

Tangy, yeasty Russian buckwheat blini make wonderful wrappers for an assortment of breakfast or brunch treats in this casual, serve-yourself menu. Make a stack of the blini and keep them warm, wrapped in a heavy napkin inside a heated serving dish. Place them on the table along with a covered baking dish that you've filled with creamy scrambled eggs; small bowls of sour cream, crumbled bacon, chopped chives, and salmon or whitefish caviar; a plate of smoked salmon, cod, whitefish, or trout; sliced cheeses; assorted jams; and soft butter.

Let each breakfaster take a blini and top it to taste with any combination of the ingredients you've set out. The blini can be folded and eaten by hand, like a soft taco, or cut up and eaten with a knife and fork.

Offer chilled stewed prunes along with serve-yourself pitchers of fruit juice. Have steaming pots of coffee and strong tea on hand. For a special Russian touch, serve the tea in tall, heavy glasses set in metal holders.

For an especially elegant old-world look, cover the table with a heavy, luxurious deep burgundy or gold cloth, or use your finest antique lace. Pull out all those ornate old silver or other metal serving trays, and your heaviest silver cutlery. Conjure up the mood of the *dacha* with some *balalaika* music and place a grouping of Russian nesting dolls or other folk carvings at the center of the table.

Phillip Ennis

BUCKWHEAT
BLINI

1 package active dry yeast

½ cup warm water

2 cups milk, heated just until lukewarm

1 cup all-purpose flour

1 cup buckwheat flour

3 eggs, separated

4 tablespoons (½ stick) unsalted butter, melted

1 tablespoon sugar

½ teaspoon salt

In a small bowl, dissolve the yeast in the water. Let it sit for about 5 minutes, until foamy.

In a mixing bowl, stir the yeast into 1 cup of the milk. With a fork, beat in ½ cup each of the flours to make a smooth, thick batter. Cover and let the batter rise at warm room temperature for about 1½ hours, until it has increased in volume and is very bubbly.

Beat the egg yolks until smooth and lemon-colored. Beat in the remaining milk, the butter, sugar, and salt, then beat in the remaining flours. Gradually beat this mixture into the already risen batter until thoroughly blended. Cover the batter and let it rise about 1 hour more.

Beat the egg whites until they form soft peaks. Gently but thoroughly fold them into the batter.

Heat a large, heavy skillet or griddle over moderate to high heat and grease it lightly. Ladle the batter onto the skillet to form 5- to 6-inch pancakes. Turn the blini when their undersides are browned, about 1 minute, reducing the heat if they seem to be browning too quickly; flip them with a spatula and cook their other sides. Keep the blini warm in a napkin-lined, heated dish while you cook the remainder.

Makes 6 servings.

Fred Lyon/Wheeler Pictures

BREAKFAST & BRUNCH BY THE SEASON

WINTER BREAKFAST FOR FOUR

FRESH ORANGE JUICE

OATMEAL WITH RAISINS, DATES, OR BANANAS

HANGTOWN FRY

THICK-SLICED SOURDOUGH TOAST

COFFEE

HOT MILK WITH HONEY

To fortify you and your family during the coldest winter days, serve a breakfast that is unabashedly hearty. Start out with steaming bowls of oatmeal topped with raisins, chopped dates, or sliced bananas. Move on to the Hangtown Fry featured here, a scramble full of crisp bacon and plump oysters, accompanied by thick slices of buttered sourdough toast and steaming mugs of coffee or hot milk with honey.

Set the table in the kitchen, for extra warmth; even if the quarters are slightly cramped, it's better to huddle close near the stove. Tune in a favorite radio station—one that gives frequent weather reports might be a wise choice. Use your everyday plates, and heavy mugs that hold in the heat and warm the hands. Place a jaunty pitcher of irises or tulips on the table to defy the cold winds and send the message that spring isn't too far away.

HANGTOWN FRY

4 strips bacon

1 medium onion, coarsely chopped

1 small bell pepper, coarsely chopped

¼ pound fresh button mushrooms, cut into ¼-inch slices

4 tablespoons (½ stick) unsalted butter

1 (8-ounce) jar freshly shucked medium oysters (about 12 oysters), thoroughly drained

10 eggs, lightly beaten

Salt and freshly ground black pepper

In a large skillet, sauté the bacon over moderate heat until crisp. Remove the bacon and drain on paper towels, leaving the fat in the skillet. Add the onion, pepper, and mushrooms to the skillet and sauté them until they are only lightly browned, about 3 minutes. With a slotted spoon, remove the vegetables to drain on paper towels. Discard the fat and wipe out the skillet.

In the same skillet, melt the butter over moderate to low heat. Add the oysters and sauté them gently just until they begin to firm up, about 2 minutes. Add the eggs and vegetables and crumble in the bacon. Cook the eggs, stirring and scraping gently, until they form thick, creamy curds. Season to taste with salt and plenty of black pepper and serve at once.

Makes 4 servings.

SPRING BRUNCH FOR FOUR

PLATTER OF FRESH SPRINGTIME FRUITS

ASPARAGUS AND FINES HERBES FRITTATA

CROISSANTS WITH BUTTER AND JAM

COFFEE AND TEA

Celebrate the season of renewal with a menu that takes advantage of the outstanding produce available in the market. Asparagus is one of springtime's greatest gifts to cooks, and it's featured here in an oven-baked frittata that you can serve hot, at room temperature, or even cold. Round out the menu with a selection of fresh springtime fruits—raspberries, strawberries, navel oranges, and a pineapple—arranged on a platter in a beautiful display.

Cover the table with a white or pale pastel linen cloth, and set it with your prettiest china: A floral pattern is most appropriate for this time of year. Fill a matching pitcher, or a delicate vase, with a springtime bouquet: gladioli, daisies, peonies, or other bright, robust blossoms. Throw the windows open to let in the sunshine and breezes.

ASPARAGUS & FINES HERBES FRITTATA

2 tablespoons unsalted butter

1 tablespoon olive oil

1 pound fresh asparagus, trimmed and cut diagonally into ¼-inch-thick slices

1 shallot, finely chopped

6 eggs

½ cup plus 2 tablespoons grated Parmesan cheese

2 teaspoons chopped fresh parsley

2 teaspoons chopped fresh chives

2 teaspoons chopped fresh tarragon

¼ teaspoon salt

¼ teaspoon black pepper

R. Hamilton Smith/Manhattan Views

Preheat the oven to 350°F.

In a 10-inch ovenproof skillet, melt the butter with the olive oil over moderate to high heat. Add the asparagus and shallot and sauté until the asparagus is tender but still crisp, about 2 minutes. Spread the asparagus evenly in the skillet.

In a mixing bowl, beat the eggs thoroughly, then stir in the ½ cup of Parmesan, herbs, salt, and pepper. Pour this mixture over the asparagus. Put the skillet in the oven and bake until the frittata is set, its top still slightly moist, about 20 minutes. Sprinkle the top with the remaining Parmesan and brown the frittata under the broiler for 1 to 2 minutes.

Serve the frittata directly from the skillet, cut into wedges, or loosen its edges with a narrow spatula and transfer it to a platter. Serve hot, at room temperature, or cold.

Makes 4 servings.

SUMMER BREAKFAST FOR FOUR

FRESHLY SQUEEZED FRUIT JUICE

FRUIT MUESLI

ICED TEA OR COFFEE

During the season when "the livin' is easy," don't be hard on yourself by cooking an elaborate breakfast. And don't be hard on your digestion with a morning meal that's too hearty for the summer heat.

Take advantage of plump, juicy, cooling summer fruits. Feature them in an easy-to-make muesli that—with its whole grains and creamy yogurt—satisfies you and offers all the nutrients you need to start the day, yet tastes light and refreshing.

Spoon the muesli into wide, shallow soup plates that you've chilled in the refrigerator for half an hour or so; decorate the top of each bowl with a simple pattern of sliced fruits that you've reserved from the muesli mixture. Chill your cereal spoons in the freezer, then take them out and wrap them in a napkin just moments before you sit down to eat; let the guests pluck their icy spoons from the napkins. For a centerpiece, fill a large glass bowl with summer fruits; any breakfasters who are still hungry can eat them after finishing their cereal.

There's really nothing else you need to complete the breakfast—except for juice and iced tea or coffee. Here's the secret to enjoying them at their best: When you brew coffee or tea during the summer, save any that you have left over and freeze it in an ice cube tray. Store the cubes in a freezer bag, then just pour freshly brewed coffee or tea over the cubes in a tall glass, for an undiluted icy drink.

F R U I T   M U E S L I

¼ cup whole wheat berries

¼ cup whole oats

1 cup whole-milk yogurt

¼ cup honey

1 tablespoon orange juice

1 apple, cored (skin left on) and coarsely grated

*1 firm ripe peach, peeled, pitted, and cut into
 ¼-inch dice*

*1 firm ripe nectarine, pitted and cut into ¼-inch
 dice*

*1 firm ripe plum, peeled, pitted, and cut into
 ¼-inch dice*

1 cup seedless red grapes, cut in halves

¼ cup coarsely chopped toasted hazelnuts

The night before serving, put the wheat and oats in a bowl and add cold water to cover them by about 1 inch. Loosely cover the bowl and leave the grains to soak overnight at room temperature.

The next morning, drain the grains thoroughly. In a mixing bowl, stir together the yogurt, honey, and orange juice. Stir in the wheat and oats, the fruit, and the hazelnuts. Chill in the refrigerator for about 1 hour before serving.

Makes 4 servings.

Fred Lyon/Wheeler Pictures

AUTUMN MENU FOR FOUR

MIXED ORANGE AND GRAPEFRUIT SALAD

SWEET CORN PANCAKES

WITH WHIPPED BUTTER AND MAPLE SYRUP

SAUSAGE OR BACON

COFFEE WITH WHOLE CINNAMON STICKS

As the leaves turn, the nights begin to draw in, and the mornings start in darkness, serve a menu that sustains the body and spirit while it reflects the glowing, burnished colors of autumn.

Good sweet corn is now available well into the fall, but if you're not satisfied with what the store has to offer, by all means use canned corn for these pancakes. Serve them with whipped butter (either purchased that way or briefly whirred in your food processor) and the best maple syrup you can buy.

Set the table with dishware in earthy tones: browns, deep reds, and golds against a deep brown or gold tablecloth or plain, polished wood. Serve coffee in hearty mugs, and place a whole cinnamon stick in each for a subtle accent of flavor. Take an early morning walk outdoors to gather a colorful bouquet of autumn leaves; pile them in a wide, shallow bowl, or directly on the table, for your centerpiece. If it's close to Thanksgiving, and you have decorative gourds and multicolored ears of corn in the house, by all means add them to the arrangement. Put some good old folk music on the record player: A Woody Guthrie album adds the perfect glow.

SWEET CORN PANCAKES

1⅓ cups all-purpose flour

½ cup fine yellow cornmeal

2 tablespoons brown sugar

2 teaspoons baking powder

½ teaspoon salt

2 tablespoons unsalted butter, softened

2 eggs

1½ cups milk

¾ cup cooked corn kernels, drained

In a mixing bowl, stir together the flour, cornmeal, sugar, baking powder, and salt. With a pair of table knives or a pastry cutter, cut in the butter.

In a separate bowl, beat the eggs thoroughly. Stir in the milk.

Stir the egg mixture into the dry ingredients until the batter is smooth. Fold in the corn.

Heat a large skillet or griddle over moderate to high heat and grease it lightly. Spoon the batter onto the skillet to make pancakes about 6 inches across. Fry them until their surface is covered with bubbles, lowering the heat if necessary to keep them from browning too quickly. Carefully flip them with a spatula and fry until their other sides are browned. Serve immediately.

Makes 4 servings.

HOLIDAY BREAKFASTS & BRUNCHES

CHRISTMAS BREAKFAST FOR FOUR

CRANBERRY OR ORANGE JUICE

SCRAMBLED EGGS

WITH CHIVE AND ROASTED BELL PEPPER GARNISH

CHRISTMAS FRUITCAKE MUFFINS

COFFEE, TEA, AND MILK

Make breakfast simple on Christmas morning. After all, you don't want an elaborate meal to get in the way of the family's enjoyment of gift-opening.

This menu is designed to start Christmas Day off fuss-free, yet in the proper festive mood. A simple dish of scrambled eggs takes on the appropriate holiday colors when topped with a garnish of chopped fresh chives and diced roasted red bell peppers (either freshly roasted or canned). Your favorite plump sausages, seared under the broiler, add to the air of feasting. Easily prepared Christmas Fruitcake Muffins, hot from the oven, offer the familiar tastes of the season.

A number of manufacturers make special Christmas dishware, with decorative borders of holly, Santas, gaily decked trees, or other symbols of the holiday. Any of these are perfect to use throughout the holiday season; feel free to substitute your finest, most festive china. Lay out your best linen table cloth, or one in a suitable holiday pattern or a solid bright red or green. A grouping of holly, favorite tree ornaments, pine sprigs, and cones, and stout red or green Christmas candles makes the perfect centerpiece.

Let the family relax on Christmas morning: robes, nightgowns, and pajamas are appropriate attire. Play a record of Christmas carols to complete the holiday mood.

Courtesy Wolfermans

124

CHRISTMAS FRUITCAKE MUFFINS

1½ cups all-purpose flour

¼ cup brown sugar

1 tablespoon baking powder

¼ teaspoon salt

1 egg, lightly beaten

½ cup milk

4 tablespoons (½ stick) unsalted butter, melted

½ cup diced red and green candied cherries

½ cup mixed diced candied pineapple

½ cup seedless raisins

2 teaspoons grated lemon zest

2 teaspoons grated orange zest

Preheat the oven to 400°F.

In a mixing bowl, stir together the flour, sugar, baking powder, and salt. In a separate bowl, stir together the egg, milk, and butter, then stir them into the dry ingredients to make a lumpy batter. Fold in the remaining ingredients.

Spoon the batter into greased muffin cups, filling them about two-thirds full. Bake until well risen, golden, and a thin wooden toothpick inserted into the center of a muffin comes out clean, 25 to 30 minutes.

Makes 12 muffins.

HANUKKAH BRUNCH FOR EIGHT

HANUKKAH GELT MINI POTATO PANCAKES

WITH SWEET VANILLA SOUR CREAM AND

CINNAMON APPLE SAUCE WITH BRANDIED RAISINS

MILK, FRUIT JUICE, COFFEE OR TEA

One of the traditions of the Jewish Festival of Lights is the giving of *Hanukkah gelt*, gold coins that symbolize a wish for prosperity in the year to come. The favorite food of the holiday is *latkes*, potato pancakes that are fried in a little oil—the oil recalling the miraculous single drum of oil that kept the eternal light burning in the temple for eight days and nights when it should have lasted only for one.

Traditionally, Hanukkah is celebrated every evening at sundown. But, for a special holiday breakfast or brunch, you can have friends (or your children's friends) over and serve these small potato pancakes, whose size and golden color are meant to suggest Hanukkah gelt. Accompany them with lightly sweetened sour cream and a fresh apple sauce spiced with cinnamon and brandied raisins, and serve steaming mugs of your favorite spiced tea.

Decorate the table with cloth, napkins, and dishes in the holiday colors of blue and white. At each setting, place a *dreidel*—the special Hanukkah top with Hebrew letters on each of its four sides, for an old-fashioned game of chance.

HANUKKAH GELT MINI POTATO PANCAKES

8 medium potatoes, peeled and quartered

1 medium onion, grated

2 large eggs, well beaten

2 tablespoons all-purpose flour

1½ teaspoons salt

½ teaspoon freshly ground white pepper

Vegetable oil for frying

Place the potatoes in a large bowl of cold water. Leave them to soak for at least 1 hour, then drain them thoroughly, pat them dry, and shred them coarsely.

In a mixing bowl, toss the potato shreds with the grated onion. Stir in the eggs, then dust the mixture with the flour, salt, and pepper and stir until thoroughly blended.

Heat about a ¼-inch layer of oil in a large, heavy skillet over moderate to high heat. Drop the potato mixture in scant tablespoons into the oil to form small, round pancakes. Fry them until they are deep golden brown on their undersides, no more than about 2 minutes, then carefully turn them and fry the other sides. Remove the pancakes to drain on paper towels, then transfer them to a tray in the oven to keep warm. Repeat with the remaining mixture, adding more oil if necessary. Serve the pancakes with Sweet Vanilla Sour Cream and Cinnamon Apple Sauce.

Makes 8 servings.

SWEET VANILLA SOUR CREAM

1 cup sour cream

1 tablespoon confectioner's sugar

½ teaspoon vanilla extract

Place all the ingredients in a mixing bowl and stir until thoroughly blended. Cover and chill until serving.

Makes 1 cup.

Peter W. Gonzalez/Manhattan Views

CINNAMON APPLE SAUCE WITH BRANDIED RAISINS

Make this simple apple sauce the night before you plan to serve it.

8 medium-sized crisp apples, peeled, cored, and
cut into 1-inch chunks

½ cup water

2 tablespoons brown sugar

½ cup brandy

½ cup seedless raisins

1 teaspoon cinnamon

Put the apples, water, and sugar in a medium saucepan. Cover the pan and cook the apples over low heat just until they begin to soften, about 20 minutes.

Meanwhile, bring the brandy to a boil in a small saucepan. Put the raisins in a small bowl, pour the hot brandy over them and leave them to soak.

Transfer the apples to a processor, add the cinnamon, and turn the machine on and off until the apples are coarsely pureed. Transfer the apple sauce to a large bowl. Drain the brandy from the raisins, and stir the raisins into the sauce. Cover the bowl and chill in the refrigerator for 2 to 3 hours.

Makes about 4 cups.

HOLIDAY HORS D'OEUVRE BUFFET BRUNCH FOR TWENTY-FOUR

FRESH FRUIT JUICES

PLATTER OF ASSORTED FRESH SEASONAL FRUITS

SCRAMBLED EGGS IN BAKED POTATO SHELLS

MINIATURE SAUSAGE LINKS OR PATTIES

MINI CROISSANTS

ASSORTED MINI MUFFINS

FRESHLY BREWED COFFEE & TEA

Sometimes you want to create a splendid splash with a weekend meal for friends, and this gala brunch is the ideal way to do it. Throw it late on a Sunday morning and you'll have all day Saturday for leisurely preparation, Sunday afternoon for cleanup, and Sunday evening for recuperation.

This menu ensures that the preparation, serving, cleanup, and recuperation won't require much of your time. Every dish is designed as easy-to-handle finger food: Platters of fresh seasonal fruits cut into bite-sized pieces, scrambled eggs served in little baked potato shells, small sausage links or patties, and tiny croissants or muffins.

A recipe follows for scrambled eggs in potato shells. For the fruit, simply cut up large fruits and arrange them with seasonal berries in an attractive display; you might want to spear a number of them with toothpicks for easy serving.

For the croissants, follow the recipe on page 35, but cut the rolled-out dough into smaller triangles 3 to 4 inches (7½ to 10 centimeters) on a side; then roll them up, let them rise, and bake according to the recipe, allowing 5 to 10 minutes less baking time. You can also make miniature muffins out of any of the recipes in this book (see index), using one of the mini muffin tins available in well-stocked kitchen stores; bake them at the same temperature but, as with the croissants, decrease the baking time by 5 to 10 minutes.

Set up a large table from which to serve the buffet. To keep the fruits and juices cold, set the platters and pitchers in a large tub or other deep container filled with crushed ice. Have a large chafing dish on hand to keep the egg-filled potato shells and the sausages hot. Put the croissants and muffins straight from the oven into wide, shallow baskets lined with large kitchen towels, and fold the corners of the towels up over the breads to keep them warm. Set out large dishes of butter and pots of assorted jams. To keep from having to brew fresh coffee and tea continuously, it's worthwhile to rent a pair of good-sized urns to hold the beverages.

Stack mugs for the drinks near the urns at one end of the table, and small salad plates for the food at the other along with forks and napkins. Clear plenty of space around the living room and dining room for your guests to sit, and make sure there are also sufficient surfaces upon which to rest their plates if they choose to stand.

SCRAMBLED EGGS IN BAKED POTATO SHELLS

24 small baking potatoes, scrubbed clean

Vegetable oil

Salt

24 tablespoons (3 sticks) unsalted butter

36 eggs

Freshly ground black pepper

1 pound sharp cheddar cheese, grated

¾ cup chopped fresh chives or parsley, for garnish

Preheat the oven to 400°F.

Lightly rub the potatoes with the oil and sprinkle them lightly with salt. Place them on a baking tray and bake them until done, 45 minutes to 1 hour depending on size. Remove the potatoes from the oven.

When the potatoes are cool enough to handle, halve them lengthwise. With a sharp spoon, scoop out the flesh from each half, leaving a shell about ¼ inch thick; reserve the flesh for another recipe.

In a small saucepan or skillet, melt 8 tablespoons of the butter. Brush the insides of the potato shells with the butter and return the shells to a 400°F oven until they turn golden brown inside, about 20 minutes.

Meanwhile, break the eggs into the largest mixing bowl you have. Beat well with a good-sized wire whisk. (Or break the eggs in several batches into smaller bowls and beat them.)

Melt the remaining butter over moderate to low

heat in the largest skillet or saucepan you have, or 2 or 3 smaller skillets or pans. Add the eggs and cook them, stirring and scraping frequently, until they form soft, creamy curds. Season to taste with salt and pepper.

Spoon the scrambled eggs into the baked potato shells. Sprinkle the cheese over the eggs. Garnish with chives or parsley and serve immediately.

Makes 24 servings.

Hing/Norton

NEW YEAR'S RESOLUTION BREAKFAST FOR TWO

FRESHLY SQUEEZED RUBY GRAPEFRUIT JUICE

CARROT-POPPY SEED MUFFINS

WITH WHIPPED CREAM CHEESE

MOCHA-JAVA COFFEE

It's the morning after the biggest bash of the year. Even if you *behaved* last night, you probably still feel that you've been living it up just a tad too much. It's a morning for resolutions, for starting the new year off on a firm new footing.

Frankly, you don't feel much like cooking this morning, but you probably have the energy to squeeze some juice, grind some coffee, and maybe stir up a batch of muffins. Sounds like three very basic courses, and fairly frugal—after all, especially after last night's indulgences, resolution number one must be to watch the waistline. Grapefruit juice is a must, but squeeze it from a *ruby* grapefruit, to add a bright, rosy tint to the drink. And why not lay in a special blend of coffee? Mocha-Java, with its complementary mixture of rich and sharp, mellow and full-bodied flavors, tastes excellent black, which is probably how you're going to be taking it today.

Your New Year's muffins aren't just any muffins. They're flecked with bright orange carrot shreds and rich, dark poppy seeds. The seeds, in some Eastern European cultures, are symbolic of wealth—an appropriate wish to start the new year on. And this combination of ingredients is a healthy one, in keeping with your new regimen—however long you stick to it! If you want to indulge a bit, split the muffins and spread them with some whipped cream cheese.

In an appropriately ascetic spirit, set the table with plain glass or white china plates. You probably can't face any bright patterns today, anyway. No music, no television, no newspaper, no fancy decorations. Wear your most comfortable pajamas, robe, or nightgown.

CARROT-POPPY SEED MUFFINS

½ cup all-purpose flour

½ cup whole-wheat flour

¼ cup brown sugar

1½ teaspoons baking powder

¼ teaspoon salt

1 small egg, lightly beaten

½ cup low-fat milk

2 tablespoons unsalted butter, melted

⅓ cup shredded carrots

3 tablespoons poppy seeds

Preheat the oven to 375°F.

In a mixing bowl, stir together the flours, sugar, baking powder, and salt. In a separate bowl, stir together the egg, milk, and butter. Add them to the dry ingredients and stir just until a moist, lumpy batter is formed. Add the carrots and poppy seeds and quickly stir them in.

Spoon the batter into 6 greased muffin cups. Bake until the muffins are well risen and a wooden toothpick inserted into the center of one comes out dry, 20 to 25 minutes.

Makes 6 muffins.

EASTER SUNDAY BRUNCH FOR EIGHT

PLATTER OF SPRINGTIME BERRIES

EASTER EGG OMELETS WITH THREE SAUCES

SAUSAGE PATTIES

ASSORTED MUFFINS OR CROISSANTS

COFFEE, TEA, OR MILK

An Easter Sunday brunch party is the perfect way to celebrate spring's renewal. Cooking a festive celebration needn't take you much time, though, particularly since the charms of this menu lie as much in the presentation as in the foods.

The featured attraction is an Easter Egg Omelet. The recipe gets its name from the three sauces—red, green, and white—that decorate a *fines herbes* omelet (recipe on page 57) after it has been cooked. The herbes in the omelet add a fresh springtime flavor. The sauces, carefully spooned in alternating bands across the top of each individual omelet, mimic the decorative patterns of an

Easter egg. Accompany the omelets with plump sausage patties and home-baked muffins or croissants of your choice. For an extra springtime touch, you might like to offer buttered steamed asparagus spears as a vegetable garnish.

Put out your prettiest floral china, cups and saucers, and serving dishes. As a centerpiece, set out vases filled with an abundance of springtime flowers; around the vases, place small baskets filled with an assortment of dyed Easter eggs and, for the children, appropriate Easter soft toys—chicks and bunnies.

EASTER EGG OMELETS WITH THREE SAUCES

The recipe for the Fines Herbes Omelet that is the basis for this recipe appears on page 57. Have the three sauces prepared in advance and kept warm, ready to spoon onto the omelets at serving time.

8 Fines Herbes Omelets (recipe on page 57)

Tomato-Tarragon Sauce (recipe follows)

Spinach Cream Sauce (recipe follows)

Mornay Sauce (recipe follows)

As each omelet is completed, put it on a heated serving plate and keep it warm in a low oven.

When all the omelets are done, dress them with the sauces. Carefully spoon the three sauces across each omelet in alternating bands of color. Then, with a small spoon, carefully place dots of contrasting sauces on top of each band to complete the Easter egg effect.

Jerry Howard/Positive Images

TOMATO-TARRAGON
SAUCE

2 tablespoons olive oil

1 medium garlic clove, finely chopped

1 large shallot, finely chopped

1 (28-ounce) can crushed tomatoes

1 tablespoon double-concentrate tomato paste

1 tablespoon sugar

2 teaspoons finely chopped fresh tarragon leaves

¾ teaspoon salt

In a large saucepan or skillet, heat the olive oil over medium heat. Add the garlic and shallot and sauté until tender, about 2 minutes.

Add all the remaining ingredients, bring the sauce to a boil, then simmer briskly, until fairly thick, about 15 minutes.

Pass the sauce through a fine sieve, pressing it through with a wooden spoon. Return it to the pan and continue simmering until the sauce has a thick coating consistency, about 5 minutes more.

Makes 8 servings.

Jerry Howard/Positive Images

SPINACH CREAM SAUCE

2 pounds spinach, washed and stemmed

¾ cup heavy cream

½ teaspoon salt

¼ teaspoon white pepper

⅛ teaspoon ground nutmeg

Bring a large saucepan of water to a boil. Add the spinach and cook it for about 3 minutes, until tender. Drain the spinach thoroughly and rinse it under cold running water; then drain again, pressing out all the liquid with your hand.

Put the spinach in a processor with the remaining ingredients. Process until smoothly pureed. Pass the puree through a fine sieve back into the saucepan. Continue cooking the puree over low heat until it is heated through and has a thick coating consistency, about 5 minutes.

Makes 8 servings.

MORNAY SAUCE

2 cups milk

4 tablespoons (½ stick) unsalted butter

4 tablespoons all-purpose flour

½ cup grated Parmesan cheese

Salt and freshly ground white pepper

In a medium saucepan, heat the milk over medium heat until hot but not boiling.

In a separate heavy saucepan, melt the butter over medium heat. Sprinkle in the flour, stirring constantly to avoid lumps, and continue stirring, letting the mixture cook for 2 to 3 minutes without browning.

With a wire whisk or a wooden spoon, gradually stir the hot milk into the flour-and-butter paste. Raise the heat slightly and bring the mixture to a boil, stirring constantly. Reduce the heat and simmer for about 5 minutes more, stirring in the Parmesan cheese as the sauce begins to thicken. Taste the sauce and add salt and white pepper as necessary. Continue simmering until the sauce has a thick consistency and coats the spoon.

Makes 8 servings.

BRUNCHES FROM FOUR GREAT RESTAURANTS

BRUNCH FOR FOUR AT THE RITZ-CARLTON, BOSTON

THE RITZ-CARLTON FIZZ

CREAMED FINNAN HADDIE ON TOAST

BLUEBERRY MUFFINS RITZ-CARLTON

The weekend brunch is a glorious affair at The Ritz-Carlton, one of America's grandest hotels. Served in the ornate dining room overlooking the Boston Public Gardens, the brunch features a selection of dishes that reflect both a classic French sensibility and a hearty respect for the traditional dishes of New England. Executive Chef Jean-Francis Mots, who has led the kitchen since early 1987, recommends a menu that combines the best of both worlds.

THE RITZ-CARLTON FIZZ

This champagne cocktail is an elegant way to start a weekend brunch. If you want to be totally authentic, use the champagne of choice at The Ritz-Carlton: Perrier-Jouet Grand Brut.

4 dashes amaretto

4 dashes blue curaçao

4 dashes strained lemon juice

1 split brut champagne, chilled

4 rose petals, for garnish

Put 1 dash each of amaretto, curaçao, and lemon juice in each champagne flute. Fill each glass with champagne and float a rose petal on top.

Makes 4 servings.

CREAMED FINNAN HADDIE ON TOAST

Legend has it that finnan haddie was invented a century ago, when a warehouse full of haddock in the port of Findon, Scotland, caught fire. The resulting smoked fish was an instant success, and the local Scots named the fish "finnan," for their town, and "haddie" for the local dialect's pronunciation of "haddock."

4 cups heavy cream

2 cups milk

1½ pounds smoked haddock, bones removed, cut into 1-inch cubes

8 slices white bread

In a large saucepan, bring the cream and milk to a boil. Reduce the heat to a bare simmer, add the fish cubes and gently poach them for 4 minutes. With a slotted spoon, remove the fish pieces; keep them warm on a heated platter.

Bring the cream and milk back to a boil, then immediately lower to a brisk simmer. Reduce the liquid until it thickly coats a spoon.

Meanwhile, toast the bread and cut each slice diagonally into 4 triangles. Arrange 8 triangles of toast on each serving plate.

Place the haddock pieces on top of the toast and spoon the sauce on top. Serve immediately.

Makes 4 servings.

BLUEBERRY MUFFINS RITZ-CARLTON

8 tablespoons (1 stick) unsalted butter

5 large eggs

½ cup milk

3½ cups flour, sifted before measuring

2 tablespoons plus 1 teaspoon baking powder

1½ cups sugar

⅛ teaspoon salt

4 cups fresh blueberries (or 24 ounces unsweetened frozen blueberries, defrosted)

Use 2 tablespoons of the butter to coat 12 muffin molds and line the molds with paper baking cups.

In a small saucepan over medium heat, melt the remaining butter.

In a mixing bowl, beat the eggs until well blended. Stir in the melted butter and the milk.

In a separate large mixing bowl, stir together the flour, baking powder, ¾ cup of the sugar, and the salt. Add the egg mixture and stir just until well-blended; do not overmix, or the muffins will be tough. Fold in the blueberries.

Cover the bowl with plastic wrap and refrigerate for 2 hours.

Preheat the oven to 400°F.

Spoon the batter into the baking cups so that it mounds about ¼ inch above the top of each cup; the batter will be stiff enough not to spread out. Sprinkle the muffins generously with the remaining sugar.

Bake the muffins in the center of the oven until their tops are golden brown, 25 to 30 minutes. Serve them warm.

Makes 12 muffins.

Courtesy The McIlhenny Company

A SELECTION OF BRUNCH DISHES FROM ARNAUD'S

BRANDY MILK PUNCH

STRAWBERRIES IN PORT

BANANAS FOSTER

At Arnaud's, in the atmospheric old French Quarter of New Orleans, owner Archie Casbarian has stylishly revived the traditions established in 1918 by the restaurant's founder, Arnaud Cazenave. That means outstanding French and Creole cooking, served in an opulent, airy setting that captures the soul of the Vieux Carré.

Arnaud's menu offers seductive breakfast and brunch dishes. Several omelet and egg preparations feature New Orleans' noteworthy crayfish, along with an elaborate Amoricaine sauce. Founded on an intense lobster sauce base, it is flavored with the essence of crayfish shells, fish stock, wine, brandy, garlic, and other aromatic vegetables.

Arnaud's subtle, exquisite touches are what make the cuisine distinctive. Each of the recipes that follows—for a bracing Brandy Milk Punch to start off a weekend brunch, for Strawberries in Port, and for the traditional brunchtime dessert known as Bananas Foster—will add a truly special flair to any brunch you care to serve.

BRANDY MILK PUNCH

1½ cups milk

1½ cups half and half

9 ounces brandy

6 tablespoons simple sugar syrup

1 tablespoon vanilla extract

Nutmeg

Put half of each ingredient except the nutmeg in a cocktail shaker with ice. Shake well.

Strain the drink into 3 chilled highball glasses partially filled with ice cubes. Dust the top with nutmeg before serving. Repeat with remaining half of ingredients to make 3 more drinks.

Makes 6 servings.

STRAWBERRIES IN PORT

6 cups strawberries, hulled

¾ cup port

Whipped cream, for garnish

Toasted slivered almonds, for garnish

Place the strawberries in a serving dish and pour the port over them.

Garnish the berries with rosettes of whipped cream and slivered almonds. Serve immediately.

Makes 6 servings.

BANANAS FOSTER

1¼ tablespoons ground cinnamon

¾ tablespoon white granulated sugar

3 cups light brown sugar

6 tablespoons (¾ stick) unsalted butter

6 whole ripe bananas, peeled, halved lengthwise, then quartered

⅓ cup dark rum

¼ cup banana liqueur

6 large scoops vanilla ice cream

Stir together the cinnamon and white sugar and set aside.

In a large skillet or the pan of a chafing dish, mash together the brown sugar and butter. Place the pan over moderate heat until the mixture melts and forms a smooth caramel.

Add the banana pieces, flat sides down, and cook for about 1 minute.

Remove the pan from the heat. Add the rum (*never* add liquor while the pan is on the heat). With a long kitchen match, carefully set the rum alight. Pour the cinnamon-sugar mixture directly into the flames.

As the flames die, add the banana liqueur. Return the pan to the heat and stir well.

Place a scoop of ice cream in each of 6 wide champagne glasses. Spoon the bananas and sauce on top. Serve immediately.

Makes 6 servings.

Jeff McNamara/James Goslee III, stylist

BRUNCH FOR FOUR AT MICHAEL'S

FRESH FRUIT

JALAPEÑO BLOODY BULLS

MICHAEL'S BLT

At his restaurant filled with modern art, just four short blocks from the California shore in Santa Monica, Michael McCarty serves a cuisine he calls "Classic American-Contemporary French." He offers ultra-fresh grilled seafood, poultry, and meat dishes, decorated with mosaics of baby vegetables; exquisite just-made angel hair pastas bathed in chardonnay cream sauces; and outlandishly delicious desserts that are wonders of the pastry-maker's skill; yet all with a light California touch.

But weekend brunch at Michael's is a more casual affair. McCarty forsakes his signature Georgio Armani suits for a polo shirt and jeans, and the restaurant's spacious garden-patio is filled with equally laid-back guests enjoying such dishes as Jalapeño Bloody Bulls and Michael's BLT. Count on Michael McCarty, though, to bring his usual quality-conscious approach to even these old-fashioned favorites: only Stolichnaya vodka graces the Bulls; and only Bay's English muffins, Kentucky limestone lettuce, and the Ace variety of tomatoes will do for the sandwich.

JALAPEÑO BLOODY BULLS

Michael uses only Stolichnaya vodka in this drink. He suggests you mix up a batch and start drinking them while you make the BLTs, and continue to drink more Bloody Bulls with the sandwiches; in that case, you may want to double the recipe.

1 fresh jalapeño chili, quartered lengthwise

1 red bell pepper, quartered

1 bunch cilantro

6 ounces Worcestershire sauce

2 teaspoons freshly ground black pepper

Dash of Tabasco sauce

Salt

4 cups tomato juice

8 ounces imported Russian vodka

8 ounces canned beef consommé

4 celery stalks

2 limes, quartered

1 fresh jalapeño chili, sliced crosswise, for garnish (optional)

One day before you plan to serve the drinks, put the quartered jalapeño and bell pepper, seeds and all, into a large glass jar or pitcher with the cilantro, Worcestershire sauce, pepper, Tabasco, and salt to taste. Add the tomato juice, cover the jar, and refrigerate for 24 hours.

Before serving, pour the tomato juice through a strainer to remove the solids. Fill four 12-ounce glasses with ice. Into each glass, pour 2 ounces of vodka and 2 ounces of consommé. Top off each glass with the tomato juice. Add a celery stalk and squeeze 2 lime quarters into each glass. For those who are really daring, add a slice of jalapeño.

Makes 4 servings.

MICHAEL'S BLT

Michael uses English muffins for his BLTs—but not just any old brand. He buys Bay's English muffins; if you like, though, substitute the best English muffins you can find. Likewise, Michael uses only baby Kentucky limestone lettuce and the Ace variety of tomatoes ("They *are* ace," he says). And he suggests you make up a fresh mayonnaise, using olive oil: "The key to a BLT is the mayo; it's like a sauce."

12 (¼-inch-thick) strips slab bacon, as lean as possible

4 English muffins

½ to ¾ cup mayonnaise, preferably homemade

4 (⅓-inch-thick) slices tomato

Salt and freshly ground white pepper

4 leaves baby Kentucky limestone lettuce

On a grill or in a skillet, cook the bacon until crisp. Drain on paper towels.

Split the English muffins and toast them on both sides. Liberally paint the cut side of each muffin half with at least 1 tablespoon of mayonnaise.

Place a tomato slice on top of the mayonnaise on 4 muffin halves. Season the tomato to taste with salt and white pepper. Crisscross 3 bacon strips, like a star, on top of each tomato slice. Place a lettuce leaf on top of the bacon, and top the sandwich with the remaining muffin half. Carefully cut the sandwich in half and serve immediately.

Makes 4 servings.

Fred Lyon/Wheeler Pictures

SPA CUISINE® BRUNCH FOR FOUR AT THE FOUR SEASONS

FRESH TROPICAL FRUITS

SHRIMP AND CORN CAKES

HERB TEA OR DECAFFEINATED COFFEE

For well over a quarter century, The Four Seasons in New York City has been at the forefront of great contemporary dining. No wonder, then, that the restaurant's owners, Tom Margittai and Paul Kovi, along with chef Seppi Renggli, broke new ground yet again when, in early 1983, they decided to introduce to their menu a special new category of dishes that recognize the growing interest in food that is low in calories, low in sodium and cholesterol, yet gastronomically spectacular. They called it Spa Cuisine®, and it was an immediate success with customers and critics alike.

Seppi Renggli's Shrimp and Corn Cakes are a perfect example of this new approach to cooking. Like many of the dishes he has created for The Four Seasons, this one demonstrates not only a superb light touch but also the chef's innovative use of exotic ingredients—in this case, fish sauce and lemon grass (available from Southeast Asian markets or gourmet shops), along with jalapeño peppers and cilantro. The recipe is an excellent brunch dish, and would be wonderfully complemented by fresh tropical fruits and your favorite herb tea or Swiss water-processed decaffeinated coffee.

SHRIMP & CORN CAKES

4 tablespoons corn oil

1½ cups sliced shallots

1 cup scallion greens, cut into ¼-inch pieces

¼ cup chopped cilantro (fresh coriander), with stems and roots

2 tablespoons finely chopped lemon grass

2 teaspoons finely chopped fresh ginger

2 medium jalapeño peppers, stemmed, seeded and finely chopped

1 pound shrimp, peeled and deveined

1½ cups fresh corn

1 cup cooked white rice

3 tablespoons fish sauce (Nam Pla)

In a large skillet, heat 3 tablespoons of the oil over moderate heat. Sauté the shallots, scallions, cilantro, lemon grass, ginger, and jalapeños for 15 minutes, without browning.

Put the sautéed mixture in a processor with half the shrimp, half the corn, half the rice, and half the fish sauce. Process until it forms a coarse puree. Add the remaining shrimp, corn, rice, and fish sauce and process briefly, just until they are incorporated.

Remove the mixture from the processor and divide it into 8 equal portions. With wet hands, shape each portion into an oval patty about ½ inch thick.

Heat the remaining tablespoon of oil in a non-stick skillet over moderate heat. Sauté the patties for 3 minutes per side and serve immediately.

Makes 4 servings.

Mark Niederman

SOURCES

The following companies supply fine breakfast foods and ingredients, along with other gourmet items, by mail. Write or phone for their latest price lists and catalogs.

Balducci's
424 Avenue of the Americas
New York, NY 10011
(800) 228-2028, ext. 72
specialty foods

Bon Vivant
36425 Churchill Drive
Solon, OH 44139
(216) 248-3911
specialty foods

Community Kitchens
P.O. Box 3778
Baton Rouge, LA 70821
(800) 535-9901
preserves, coffees, teas, and other gourmet items

Dean & DeLuca
110 Greene Street, Suite 304
New York, NY 10012
(800) 221-7714
specialty foods

DeLaurenti
1435 First Avenue
Seattle, WA 98101
(206) 622-0141
specialty foods

Dimpflmeier Bakery
P.O. Box 192
Port Credit, ONT L5G 4L7
Canada
(416) 239-3031
German-style breads

Figi's
Dairy Lane
Marshfield, WI 54404
(715) 384-6101
preserves, smoked meats, and cheeses

F.H. Gillingham & Co.
16 Elm Street
Woodstock, VT 05091
(802) 457-2100

apples, maple syrup, and cheeses

Goldrush Enterprises
122 East Grand Avenue
South San Francisco, CA 94080
(800) 531-2039
sourdough bread, muffin, pancake and waffle mixes

Grandma Morgan's Gourmet Kitchen
P.O. Box 972
Lake Oswego, OR 97034
(503) 761-4303
specialty foods

Harrington's
170B-5 Main Street
Richmond, VT 05477
(802) 434-4444
meats, cheeses, and other gourmet items

Harry and David
Bear Creek Orchards
Medford, OR 97501
(503) 776-2400
fruits, preserves, smoked meats, and other gourmet items

Hawaiian Plantations
1311 Kalakaua Avenue
Honolulu, HI 96826
(800) 367-2177
pineapples, jams, jellies, and other gourmet items

House of Webster
Box 488
1013 North Second Street
Rogers, AR 72757
(501) 636-4640
preserves, biscuit mixes, bacon, and other gourmet items

Lambs Farm
P.O. Box 520
Libertyville, IL 60048
(312) 362-4636
preserves, breads, cheeses, and other gourmet items

Latta's of Oregon
P.O. Box 1377
Newport, OR 97365
(503) 265-3238
preserves, syrups, and other gourmet items

Le Gourmet Canadien
988 Elgin Avenue
Winnipeg, Manitoba R3E 1B4
Canada
(800) 665-0272
maple syrup, honey, and other gourmet items

Lindsay Farms
P.O. Box 581
Atlanta, GA 30361
(404) 233-2343
preserves

Maple Grove
167 Portland Street
St. Johnsbury, VT 05819
maple syrup, preserves, and other gourmet items

Mission Orchards
P.O. Box 6387
San Jose, CA 95150
(408) 297-5056
specialty foods

Norm Thompson
P.O. Box 3999
Portland, OR 97208
(800) 547-1160
preserves, smoked salmon, cheeses, and other gourmet items

Northwestern Coffee Mills
217 North Broadway
Milwaukee, WI 53202
(414) 276-1031
coffees and teas

Nueske Hillcrest Farm Meats
R.R. 2
Wittenberg, WI 54499
(800) 382-2266
hams, bacon, and sausages

Oakville Grocery
7856 St. Helena Highway

Oakville, CA 94562
(707) 944-8802
specialty foods

Pinnacle Orchards
441 South Fir
Medford, OR 97501
(800) 547-0227
fruits

S.E. Rykoff & Company
P.O. Box 21467
Los Angeles, CA 90021
(800) 421-9873
specialty foods

Sable & Rosenfeld
89 McCaul Street, Suite 225
Toronto, ONT M5T 2X7
Canada
(416) 595-1727
preserves, jams, and other gourmet items

Totem Smokehouse
1906 Pike Place
Seattle, WA 98101
(800) 9-SALMON
smoked salmon

Upper Canada Coffee Works & Tea Mill
534 Gordon Baker Road
Willowdale, ONT M2H 2S6
Canada
(416) 494-9700
coffees and teas

Williams-Sonoma
5750 Hollis Street
Emeryville, CA 94608
(415) 652-1555
specialty foods

Wolferman's
1900 West 47th Place
Suite 218
Westwood, KS 66205
(800) 255-0169
English muffins

Zabar's
2245 Broadway
New York, NY 10024
(800) 221-3347

RECIPE INDEX

· K I T C H E N   M E T R I C S ·

For cooking and baking convenience, the Metric Commission of Canada suggests the following for adapting to metric measurement. The table gives approximate, rather than exact, conversions.

· S P O O N S ·

¼ teaspoon = 1 milliliter
½ teaspoon = 2 milliliters
1 teaspoon = 5 milliliters
1 tablespoon = 15 milliliters
2 tablespoons = 25 milliliters
3 tablespoons = 50 milliliters

· C U P S ·

¼ cup = 50 milliliters
⅓ cup = 75 milliliters
½ cup = 125 milliliters
⅔ cup = 150 milliliters
¾ cup = 175 milliliters
1 cup = 250 milliliters

· O V E N   T E M P E R A T U R E S ·

200°F = 100°C		350°F = 180°C
225°F = 110°C		375°F = 190°C
250°F = 120°C		400°F = 200°C
275°F = 140°C		425°F = 220°C
300°F = 150°C		450°F = 230°C
325°F = 160°C		475°F = 240°C